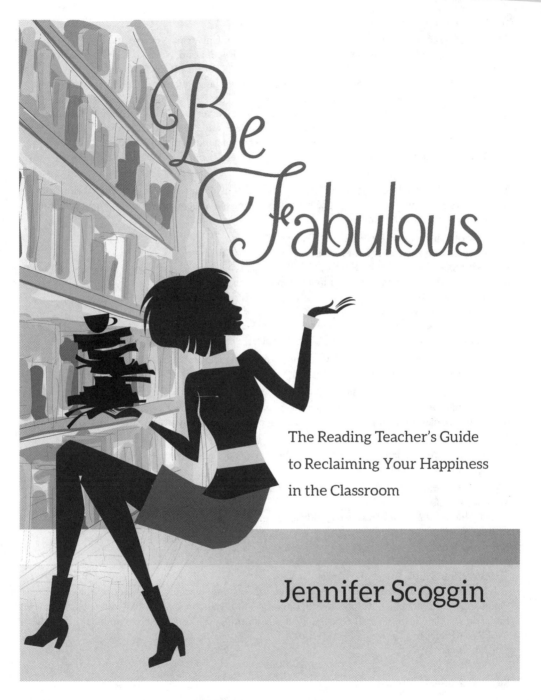

Be Fabulous

The Reading Teacher's Guide
to Reclaiming Your Happiness
in the Classroom

Jennifer Scoggin

INTERNATIONAL
Reading Association
800 BARKSDALE ROAD, PO BOX 8139
NEWARK, DE 19714-8139, USA
www.reading.org

The International Reading Association attempts, through its publications, to provide a forum for a wide spectrum of opinions on reading. This policy permits divergent viewpoints without implying the endorsement of the Association.

Director of Educational Resources   Shannon Fortner
Acquisitions and Development Manager   Tori Mello Bachman
Acquisitions Editor   Becky Fetterolf
Managing Editors   Christina M. Lambert and Susanne Viscarra
Digital Project Manager   Wes Ford
Editorial Associate   Wendy Logan
Creative Services/Production Manager   Anette Schuetz
Design and Composition Associate   Lisa Kochel

Cover   Design, Beth C. Ford, Glib Communications and Design; art, © Shutterstock/Lorelyn Medina, © Shutterstock/tachyglossus

The publisher would appreciate notification where errors occur so that they may be corrected in subsequent printings and/or editions.

Library of Congress Cataloging-in-Publication Data

Scoggin, Jennifer.
  Be fabulous : the reading teacher's guide to reclaiming your happiness in the classroom / Jennifer Scoggin.
    pages   cm.
  Includes bibliographical references and index.
  ISBN 978-0-87207-367-8 (alk. paper)
  1. Reading teachers—Handbooks, manuals, etc. 2. Reading teachers—Attitudes. 3. Reading—Philosophy. 4. Teaching—Philosophy. 5. Literacy—Study and teaching. 6. Reading teachers—Professional relationships. 7. Teacher–student relationships. 8. Classroom environment. I. Title.
  LB2844.1.R4S36   2014
  371.1—dc23

2014025444

Suggested APA Reference
Scoggin, J. (2014). *Be fabulous: The reading teacher's guide to reclaiming your happiness in the classroom*. Newark, DE: International Reading Association.

Behind every fabulous woman is a fabulous man, right? This book is dedicated to the three most important men in my life: Without you and your support, I wouldn't be nearly this fabulous.

Mr. Granger, you invested so much in the potential of a little girl who loved to read.

Fred, you taught me about holding my own, the importance of a firm handshake, driving greasy side down, and being a woman who contributes equally in any relationship.

Nathan, you make me a better friend, wife, mother, and teacher every day. Your unconditional love and support are fabulous.

CONTENTS

Let's Get Acquainted
Who Mrs. Mimi Is and Why You Need This Book

Let's Get Real
What Makes Teaching Difficult

Let's Get Deep
Embrace Your Teaching Philosophy

ABOUT THE AUTHOR

 **Jennifer Scoggin**, creator of the character Mrs. Mimi, began blogging about her experiences in the classroom in 2007. Select essays from her blog, It's Not All Flowers and Sausages (itsnotallflowersandsausages.blogspot.com), were turned into a book of essays called *It's Not All Flowers and Sausages: My Adventures in Second Grade* (Kaplan, 2009). Jennifer also writes for the International Reading Association's Reading Today Online blog (www.reading.org/reading-today/classroom/mrs-mimi#.U6niFPldVQF). Writing as Mrs. Mimi and connecting to teachers from around the world in such a unique manner has been one of the most unexpected joys of Jennifer's career as an educator.

Jennifer is currently a literacy consultant for LitLife as well as the director of the Connecticut branch of the company. Prior to working for LitLife, she taught both first and second grades in Harlem. She holds a doctorate in curriculum and instruction from Teachers College, Columbia University.

Jennifer lives with her husband and two fabulous children in Connecticut. When she's not reading or thinking about reading, Jennifer enjoys even more reading!

ACKNOWLEDGMENTS

First and foremost, I want to thank every teacher out there. Yes, that's right, all of you. I know that it doesn't always feel as if people understand just how hard you work and just how much you care; please know that I do. I know how fabulous you are, and I can see the fabulous you that you are on your way to becoming.

I also need to thank each and every super colleague in my life. Virtual hugs! My nearest and dearest super colleagues are not only some of my favorite people in the world but also some of the most hardworking, inspiring, and, well, fabulous teachers you will ever see in action. Children are lucky to encounter these men and women during their educational careers.

Of course, I send a special shout-out to the teachers who have read and supported Mrs. Mimi all of these years. Thank you for sticking with me through two children (and my subsequent blog absence) and all the ups and downs that come along with teaching. Writing as Mrs. Mimi has been one of the most surprising and wonderful parts of my life, and that is because of you. I can't thank you enough for allowing her to grow into a huge part of who I am.

To all of my colleagues at LitLife, I never imagined that I would be lucky enough to work with such a talented, dedicated, and supportive group of people. I wish we were all in one room more often! Thank you for helping me find a path to being the educator I need and want to be at this point in my life.

And I can't forget my peeps at the International Reading Association! Lara Zeises Deloza, our deeply nerdy and wonderful virtual friendship has been such a lovely bonus in the midst of this collaboration. Thank you so much for supporting Mrs. Mimi and believing in what she has to say. I am still blown away when I think of the opportunities that you have thrown my way. Tori Bachman, Christina Lambert, Stacey Reid, Shannon Fortner, and Susanne Viscarra, thank you so much for your dedication, support, and input on this project. This work is definitely more fabulous because of you, your time, and your fabulous brains.

Last but not least, I need to send some special love to a few very important people. Mr. Granger, I wish you were here to see this. Thank you for giving me the opportunity to have this lovely life. Mom and Fred, thank you for supporting me in everything I do, even when it's too much for one person to handle. I feel so lucky that you are my parents. Nathan (the infamous Mr. Mimi), what can I say? Thank you for letting me be who I am as well as supporting who I am not yet, even when I cry about never having enough time. I love you. Lily and Charlie, my little loves, you are the joys of my life. I love you and love you and know that you are both going to be the most fabulous people. You already are to me.

Let's Get Acquainted

Who Mrs. Mimi Is and
Why You Need This Book

> *When we tell and listen to stories, we can almost feel our souls breathing fully and deeply. Our capacity to see options, to visualize possibilities, to imagine expands and we are somehow more alive.*
>
> —Michael Parent (2013, para. 2)

I have a story for you. Picture a classroom of first-grade students in Harlem. I have always referred to my students as my little friends because in the midst of the sea of insanity that I experienced while teaching in the public school system, my students were always little beacons of hope and joy. So, I want you to imagine my 20 little first-grade friends engrossed in their independent reading. (OK, maybe "engrossed" is taking it a bit far, but they were definitely more engaged than not, and it's my story, so we're just going to go with it.) One little girl, who we will call Peanut, is so involved in her own reading that she is unaware of anyone or anything around her. A diligent learner, Peanut is working tirelessly to decode each and every difficult word that she encounters in her text. I am conferring with another student at Peanut's table, trying to tune out her determined but very loud sounding out ("f –f –f—faaaaa—faaaab—faaab ewwww—faaab ewwww lus"). A few moments later, Peanut reaches the end of her book, slams it shut with a definitive bang, and declares, "Look, Mrs. Mimi, I'm learning! Can't you see?! I'm *learning*!" It was like a battle cry—a battle cry that made my eyes fill with tears and my class burst into spontaneous cheers of support and encouragement. In that moment, I thought to myself, This is why I teach; this is it right here.

I'll wait while you grab a tissue.

I have another story for you. But this time, you may want to grab a cocktail or, perhaps more appropriate, a small object to hurl across the room.

Picture a team of four oh-so-fabulous elementary teachers sitting around a table with administrators, academic coaches, and a few members of a professional development team. The teachers had been called in to a meeting to receive the message that not only were their current redundant assessments going to stay in place, but it had also been decided that a new and uber time-consuming *new* assessment was being added to the pile. Three teachers sat in stunned silence, thinking, When am I going to fit in independent reading time? How am I going to keep going with that author study? When am I supposed to teach anything at all? And the fourth teacher? Well, she just put her head down and cried.

Uplifting? Not exactly. Sound familiar? Probably. These two stories are just a brief example of the ups and downs that fill the daily lives of teachers. A wise professor once told me that the trick to finding happiness in teaching is learning how to balance out the highs and the lows. I am not certain that I have found the one and only fail-proof trick, but I do know that sharing the stories of my teaching life has made a tremendous difference in my ability to find balance.

I love a good story. I also love a good cocktail. Give me a juicy cocktail and a juicy classroom story, and I am one happy lady. In fact, these two things were literally the keys to surviving my first few years in the classroom.

Each and every Friday, I would return from dismissing my little friends to find several of my fellow super colleagues waiting in my classroom with their bags already packed. "Rough week?" I would ask, and they would nod. As a group, we would head downtown to the same place because they were expecting us and because they had free food, and you know, when you spend most of your paycheck on books and classroom supplies, free food is kind of a bonus. Did we sit around and kvetch about fellow colleagues? Yes. Did we moan and groan about particularly challenging students? Yes. Did we yell over one another to vie for the title of she-who-has-the-worst-story-of-the-week? Clearly. Eventually, my nonteacher friends would learn to not even bother calling on a Friday night because I was working.

Although, yes, the cocktails were plenty, it wasn't the cocktails that held our group together. It was the stories. After a week of holding it together and guiding our little friends through what often feels like the battlefield of today's classroom, we could finally breathe and tell our stories. War stories. There were infuriating stories of classroom interruptions, unreasonable parents, pointless meetings, and out-of-touch administrators. But there were also encouraging stories of supportive colleagues and successful students. It was not only the act of telling our own stories that felt therapeutic but also having someone actually *listen* to what we were saying and acknowledge our lived experiences. Those stories were our way of saying, I hear you. I have been there. I know what it's like. I know teaching isn't what it looks like in the movies or your dusty childhood memories of the classroom.

I returned to my classroom most Mondays with a smile on my face and a plan book full of ideas despite those times when I thought I couldn't teach another minute. I feel obligated to tell you that my little friends were a huge source of inspiration, and although at times they drove me nuts, I kept coming back for them. Of course I did. But many times, it was a Friday evening full of storytelling with my colleagues that made me feel human again and like I could return to my classroom, if only to see what stories the next week would bring.

As I gained more experience in the classroom and started to work toward a graduate degree, I found myself thinking often about the story of the teacher, the students, and those stories we share together in our classrooms. Every year, the story of my classroom and my life as a teacher changes as new characters, new conflicts, and new resolutions are introduced. Yet, I am continually frustrated by the portrayal of teachers and classroom life in movies filled with too many leather pants, overly simplistic happy endings, or poorly researched angry rants in the media.

I became intrigued with using children's literature to tap into and inspire the telling of the stories of my students. (Or at least, that's what I told my husband when he remarked on the amount of money charged to my beloved Barnes & Noble card, a.k.a. Barnsey.) How could I encourage my students as readers and writers to consume and share their own stories in ways that would expand their imaginations and sense of possibility? This questioning led me on a personal journey, too. How could I make known the story of today's classrooms? I started a blog to vent my frustrations, share my successes, and put the story of a real teacher out into the world.

This book is an extension of my blog, combining my own classroom stories with my research into what works in reading instruction, wrapped up in a package that I hope will give you—my fellow teacher super colleagues—new insight into making your classroom a thriving learning environment. It has been a deeply nerdy dream of mine for quite some time to create a resource for teachers that stands on best practices but is based in the reality of today's classrooms. In addition, and perhaps even more important, it is my hope that this book serves as a battle cry that helps you recognize the importance of your own happiness and motivates you to reinvent your classroom to become a place where you feel empowered, successful, and—dare we dream—happy.

Who Is Mrs. Mimi, Anyway?

The first word that comes to mind is *fabulous*. Mrs. Mimi, a pseudonymous persona I originally created for the purposes of writing anonymously about my own teaching experiences, is the most fabulous version of both my doctoral and teacher selves. Mrs. Mimi is witty, irreverent, current, and honest. She says what many teachers are thinking yet are unwilling to say aloud or admit in public ways. She understands the pressures of the classroom but is also schooled in the literature about best practices. She is honest about the realistic tipping point for teachers. Her voice and stories stem from various aspects of my life as an educator. After receiving a master's degree in sociology and education from Teachers College, Columbia University, I leaped into teaching first and second grades in a charter school in Harlem. I quickly realized that my true place was in a regular public school and, after one year, moved to a wonderful and challenging public school across the street. There, I met a great number of super colleagues who remain my friends today. I also came up against a large number of frustrations that inspired me to start my blog and learn more about the educational world outside of my classroom. You see, it has always been a goal of mine to someday work with young men and women as they are studying to become certified classroom teachers, so it was back to school for me.

I completed my doctoral work in curriculum and instruction at Teachers College while teaching full time over the course of the next several years. My research, among other things, focused on the identities of teachers and how these identities shift and impact classroom practice over time and in response to factors such as political change. The stories told by the participants in my study continuously echoed a similar refrain: Teacher happiness was key, and teachers were struggling to be happy. After completing my doctoral work, I moved to become a literacy consultant. I have long-term contracts in a variety of schools—no wham-bam-thank-you-ma'am professional development for me! I get to build relationships with teachers (and students) as we work to improve their literacy practices. This allows me to also think about, advocate for, and emphasize the importance of teacher happiness in real ways on a daily basis.

I created the character Mrs. Mimi in 2007 when I first began a blog about my experiences in the classroom. I was midway through my doctoral work and many years into my teaching career; it was a time when my frustrations with the classroom were at an all-time high. To be clear, my frustrations were rarely about my students, or my little friends, as I like to call them. Yes, at times, my students pushed my buttons and challenged my thinking, but that's what I signed up for when I decided to become a teacher. The frustrations that kept me awake at night were those caused by individuals outside my classroom walls: Curricular mandates that stifled my ability to meet the true needs of my students, incessant assessment that took up precious time yet never yielded data that impacted my practice in meaningful ways, and meetings that were meetings just for the sake of being meetings were the tip of the iceberg. One night, I came home ranting and raving about yet another disruption to my instruction and watched my normally attentive husband's eyes glaze over. I realized in that moment that I had officially worn him down and needed to find a new way to decompress. And thus, my blog, It's Not All Flowers and Sausages (www.itsnotallflowersandsausages.blogspot.com), was born. Clearly, I never thought anyone would read it, or I might have come up with a more logical name. It's Not All Flowers and Sausages doesn't exactly scream "education blog," now does it?

Regardless, almost immediately after writing my first post, I felt better. Simply putting my voice out into the world and venting about the often ridiculous antics that public school teachers are expected to endure helped me breathe easier and refocus on what was truly important: my students. To my surprise, people began to respond to my posts by sharing similar frustrations and adding their voices to the conversation. I was thrilled and validated and empowered. I was not alone. I felt as if I had stumbled upon something that could change the way I thought about myself and my teaching. In a deeply nerdy way, I realized that Mrs. Mimi could become a mechanism for me to combine and share my own classroom experience as well as the research that I was rapidly consuming as a doctoral student.

Quickly, Mrs. Mimi went from a goof I created late one night to a character who appealed to a large number of teachers who shared similar concerns and needed a new perspective on the same old drama or just a good laugh. The humor of Mrs. Mimi's persona allowed me to bring some much-needed levity to classroom life. As a teacher, I found it was too easy to become isolated in my own little world, and therefore, every out-of-the-classroom frustration felt larger than life and impossible to look past. Each of these occurrences threatened my happiness in significant ways on a regular basis. However, by sharing funny stories of classroom adventures as well as common frustrations, I gained a stronger voice, acknowledged the feelings of many others, and transformed my own practice and sense of empowerment. As my audience and confidence grew, so did the blog. My posts expanded to include comments on recent educational news, practical advice for common classroom practices, and funny (yet anonymous) stories of my students in addition to my original posts intended mostly to just vent. My voice was heard. My frustrations were not mine alone. I still had choices as a teacher, and those choices mattered.

How This Book Can Help You Reclaim Your Classroom Happiness

I believe firmly that "it is not possible to be a teacher without loving one's students, even realizing that love alone is not enough. It is not possible to be a teacher without loving teaching" (Freire, 1998, p. 15). These words hang above my desk. (If you can't picture it by now, I have a desk surrounded by the wise words of other educators. And piles. Of course there are piles.) It is essential for teachers to feel inspired and to love teaching again so classrooms can be revitalized as places of imagination and joy while maintaining high standards for learning. As a literacy consultant and blogger, I hear teachers from a range of schools express their frustration with the standardization of the career and practices. Many teachers have been brave enough to admit to me that they no longer feel happy at this moment in their career; they have lost the sense of joy in their work. I completely understand yet am deeply saddened by this reality for many. How can teachers be expected to instill a sense of joy into their classrooms and foster a love of learning in their students when they no longer feel these things themselves? I shudder when it is implied that standards and tests and accountability matter more than happiness and joy within the classroom. Happiness and joy do not mean a lack of rigor or solid instructional practices. They do not mean that teachers sit around playing the acoustic guitar while students string macaroni necklaces and color. Quite the contrary; happiness and joy within the classroom mean that teachers and students alike are engaged in their work in significant and dynamic ways that cannot be captured in a standard, on most tests, or in some jazzy graph.

My experience and personal research confirm that most teachers feel truly happy when they are allowed to wholly focus on meeting the needs of their students and improve their practice in ways they determine to be significant and impactful. Therefore, the primary goal for this book is to provide elementary school teachers with empowering yet practical ways to improve their own happiness as literacy educators and, therefore, their efficacy and sense of joy in the classroom. By combining personal stories of my own classroom experiences with sound, current research into best practices in literacy instruction, this book aims to serve as a professional resource for teachers who wish to reclaim or redefine who they are as educators in an increasingly standardized and controlled educational climate. In many ways, this book also aims to highlight the role of the teacher and, in particular, the happiness of the teacher, as a central factor contributing to future student success.

Organization of the Book

This book begins with a discussion of the realities of today's classroom. How did we get to this place where happiness within the classroom is rarely a consideration? In a nutshell, Chapter 1 lays all the cards out on the table, acknowledging (and venting about) what makes teaching difficult. In Chapter 2, I ask teachers to reflect on and possibly rethink their own personal philosophy of teaching to serve as a guide or road map to their own happiness within the classroom. I know that sounds like we will be lighting candles and sitting in a circle holding hands. I get it; insert eye rolling here. Although that would be lovely, the work of reconsidering your own philosophy of teaching is crucial and involves the serious task of refining and redefining your own priorities in ways that will guide your future decision making and practice.

From there, Chapters 3–6 take on more specific topics, each of which represents an issue or reality of classroom life that research (and my own experience) names as a source of stress for teachers. These topics include classroom organization and management, assessment, collegial relationships, and the use of instructional time. Finally, in Chapter 7, I lay out the case for developing and focusing on your own life as a reader as well as the need to pursue your own passions within the classroom. I like to think of this final chapter as one big pep talk that will (hopefully) inspire you to prioritize and take great strides in regaining a sense of happiness within your practice.

Before we dive in, I want to first say thank you. Thank you for showing up each and every day and giving it your all. You are fabulous and deserve to be happy. Being a teacher of reading is not an easy gig; in addition to sharing your knowledge of strategies, letter sounds, and authors, you take on and share the frustrations of students who struggle to engage with texts in joyful ways. You constantly push your instruction beyond the limits of what you thought previously possible and invest an incredible amount of energy in doing so. You are fabulous and deserve to be happy. You constantly doubt yourself, wondering whether you are doing enough, planning enough, reaching your students enough. The doubt can be painful, but it is that doubt and self-reflection that makes you a better and stronger teacher. You are fabulous, and you deserve to be happy. You consistently give of yourself. You share your reading life and preferences with your students. You share your students' favorite authors and books. Being a teacher of reading does not mean simply giving students access to instructional best practices. It means giving students access to who *you* are as a reader, a teacher, and a person.

You are fabulous, and you deserve to be happy.

CHAPTER 1

Let's Get Real

What Makes Teaching Difficult

Can teachers successfully educate children to think for themselves if teachers are not treated as professionals who think for themselves?

—Diane Ravitch (2010, p. 67)

I am a teacher, and I love my job. Truly, I do. However, lately, I often say, "I love my job," more as a reminder to myself—a mantra, if you will—than a declaration of unwavering contentment with my chosen profession. I figure I need to do one of two things: suck it up and invest in a quality cape because teachers are truly superheroes, or call it a day and join the circus. This is because on most days, I feel equal parts superhero and circus act. You know, yelling, "I can save the world," while simultaneously contorting myself into a human pretzel who must bend to the whims of every person out there who ever had an opinion about education. (For you nonteachers, we in the business call that Wednesday.)

Are you tired yet? If you are a teacher (or at least aspire to the greatness that is teaching), then the answer to that question is most likely a resounding yes. Teaching is hard. It fills my brain and my heart at almost every moment. It is exhausting, especially if you do it well. My mother taught for 41 years, so I know firsthand that this is nothing new. Yet, somehow, teaching in today's classroom seems slightly more intense, more tiring, and more frustrating than in classrooms of any other time. Well, if you ever feel like no one else notices, know that I see you and am aware of how hard you are working.

What I am trying to say is that *every* single day, teachers are amazing champions of learning who work tirelessly to push children to succeed and grow as readers, writers, mathematicians, scientists, historians, and artists. Yet, *every* single day, teachers also steel themselves to deal with an onslaught of tasks that are deemed "essential" yet seem to impact instruction in no real productive ways. There is an increasing number of demands placed on the teacher that are in addition to classroom instruction and, sadly, are often moved to be *in place of* wonderful classroom instruction. There is only so much time in the day, and currently we teachers are being pulled in too many directions. There is pressure to create, collect, and analyze data; pressure to communicate and work closely with parents; pressure to learn the new Common Core State Standards; pressure to master a new curriculum; pressure to contribute to after-school endeavors.... Need I go on? Notice that I have yet to mention any true instructional pressures, such as meeting the needs of individual students, staying current with new literature, refining our methods, or researching new best practices (a.k.a. the nerdily fun stuff).

If the world worked correctly, teachers would be showcased as the rock stars we truly are, and perform our daily routines in ways that highlight our fabulousness. We would all have our own private wind machine (à la Beyoncé) or glitter cannon for those moments when we walk down the hall to pick up our students from gym class. We would have a teachers' lounge that actually looks like someplace where people, you know, *lounge*, rather than someplace where mismatched, uncomfortable furniture and junky appliances go to die. We would all have a Keurig in our classrooms with an unlimited supply of those pod thingamajigs. We would have theme music to accompany our successes. We would get a voice at the mighty decision-making table that is responsible for shaping our daily classroom lives and the direction that our amazing profession is taking. We would be asked to participate as essential contributors to the conversations taking place about evaluation, instruction, standards, and assessment. You know, *that* pesky little stuff.

I have learned the delicate balance of surviving the emotional ebbs and flows of teaching by riding the wave of the highs and the lows—knowing that the most difficult day with my little friends is usually followed closely by some of the most successful days. However, my little friends are still a challenge. Pushing myself professionally is a challenge. Staying current with new ideas is a challenge. But those are all challenges that I welcome. I embrace them. I feel lucky that I have found a career that involves so much to engage my mind. These challenges certainly make teaching hard, but they are not what makes teaching in today's classroom feel like climbing up the down escalator while people throw rotten eggs in your face.

It's Time to Get Down and Dirty

So, let's get real. Let's talk about what makes teaching truly difficult, shall we? (Pardon me while I drag out my soapbox. *Ahem.*)

Students, and meeting the needs of our students, are not what make teaching so difficult. As I said before, they can be challenging, but they are the challenge that we signed up for, that we welcome, that keeps our professional juices flowing. The things that make teaching truly difficult and, at times, feel unbelievably cruel and punitive exist outside the walls of our classrooms. They are things that have no business invading our precious space with small children: people in suits who carry iPads we can't afford to buy our students, and shake their heads in undeserving judgment, then scurry off to secret rooms where they decide our fate in the form of high-stakes evaluations and assessments. A fickle public who jumps on the media bandwagon that largely berates teachers and paints pictures of our work that are often demoralizing. Restrictive curricular mandates that dictate how we are going to work with our students, as if a one-size-fits-all solution in a box exists or is even desirable. Let's talk a bit more about these struggles, shall we? (Feel free to grab a beverage of your choice and pull up a bar stool. I feel a Friday afternoon venting session coming on.)

The Outsiders

Is it just me, or does it *still* seem as if everyone who is in a position of power to make significant change in the educational landscape has little to no experience in an actual classroom? Am I the only one who thinks this is pure insanity? Although I think it is nice that people outside

> Historically, teachers have never been an important source of information for educational change....Most commonly, teachers enact the techniques determined by others to be efficacious for meeting goals that teachers also have had little role in defining. (Llorens, 1994, p. 3)

of the classroom care about what happens in our public schools, I am less certain that any old outsider is able to put forward an informed opinion. Historically, many large-scale attempts at school reform have done little to substantially alter the fabric of schools (things like chronological age grouping, letter grades, and timed class periods) and have failed to make a profound impact on popular perceptions of teachers or assumptions about the nature of education (Evans, 2001; Payne, 1998; Tyack & Cuban, 1995). So, why do we allow outsiders to continue to tinker around with our system? We certainly don't need more cooks in the kitchen. We need the *right* cooks in the kitchen—the cooks who have had years of experience.

> The current obsession with making our schools work like a business...threatens to destroy public education. Who will stand up to the tycoons and politicians and tell them so? (Ravitch, 2010, p. 222)

Far too often, teachers are viewed as transmitters of policy and curricula rather than active participants in the production of knowledge and solutions (Darling-Hammond, 1997). As a result of this limiting perception of teachers, we continue to look toward those outside of the classroom for guidance and direction, a reality that places too much power in the hands of those who are not intimately involved with the actual practice of educating children. A prime example of the power of the outsider that blows my mind was a televised talk about education hosted by a major network. This program, the intention of which was to debate the current state of education in our nation, had a panel of "experts" that included the CEO of a large company, the chancellor of a large public school district, a *musician*, a former secretary of education, and the president of the American Federation of Teachers. That's it: one stage full of people talking about the state of education and five chairs, none of which was occupied by an actual teacher. Did some of those individuals earn a place in the conversation? Sure. Did anyone think for just a moment that maybe, just maybe, they should put an *actual teacher* on the panel of individuals discussing the challenges and potential solutions for today's educational landscape, particularly considering that teachers will most likely be the ones to carry out said solutions? Evidently not. This discussion was hosted by a major network, so one can only assume that the names on this panel had to be hashed out in depth, and it was apparently decided that teachers did not earn a voice in this conversation. A popular musician, yes.

Teachers, no. Perhaps if we sang our opinions, we could swing the vote in our favor next time.

Can I also just say that I have had enough with listening to people compare education with a business, and I can no longer tolerate listening to businesspeople pontificate about how we might make our system more efficient and driven by competition? For those suit-and-tie types, I have six words for you: *I don't work in a business!* I work in a school. Schools are not businesses. Children are not products. Teachers are not workers on an assembly line. We are part of a complicated social system built on relationships between teachers and students, schools and families, families and communities.

For some reason, education and a fascination with efficiency have gone hand in hand for quite some time, which is perhaps why the insights of those in positions of political power are continuously privileged above those who have true educational expertise (Aronowitz & Giroux, 1993; Dirkswager, 2002; Llorens, 1994; McDonald, 1992; Rousmaniere, 1997). Obviously, schools need a well-managed budget and benefit from cutting wasteful expenditures, but in my mind, that is where the comparison with a business can and should stop. I would never *dare* to walk into a corporate office and begin to publicly criticize their work and tell people how they should do their jobs. I would never assume that because I have been to a place of business that I necessarily know how to run it better than those who currently do. I wish there was a similar level of respect for the knowledge possessed by teachers as well as the complex work we do on a daily basis. How can we ever expect teachers to foster leadership potential, develop problem-solving skills, or encourage creative thinking in our students if we don't allow teachers to do these things themselves?

The Flip-Floppers and Finger-Pointers

My husband sometimes wonders why teachers feel as if they have to work so hard to prove to everyone how difficult their job truly is. From time to time, he would come to our Friday afternoon gatherings at the watering hole and marvel at our need to share our struggles in such a detailed fashion with one another. I have always done this because it feels as if no one truly understands the scope of what teachers do on a daily basis. They just don't get it. Now, I certainly don't *get* the daily life of a doctor beyond what I see on television. However, although I am a dedicated fan of *Grey's Anatomy*, I would never presume to fully understand the medical profession. If only the general public held educators in the same esteem. Many people feel overly familiar with the teaching profession as a result of their own years in the classroom and therefore take for granted what it means to be a teacher and the work involved in running a classroom successfully (Britzman, 1991). It isn't all about organizing crayons and making sure the paper tray is filled.

Perhaps this overfamiliarity with the role of the teacher is what allows people to feel justified to love us and hate us, often at the same time. When a teacher produces positive results as measured by a test, the public loves that teacher, her teaching style, her methods. That teacher is a good teacher. When another teacher, or even the same one, produces less dynamic test results, regardless of the context in which she teaches or the effectiveness of that test to truly measure any sort of progress, that teacher is deemed terrible or ineffective or lazy. That teacher is a bad teacher. We are good or evil, rarely anything in between. A study of the images of "the teacher" that are prevalent in the 20th century supports this idea (Joseph & Burnaford, 1994). It was found that the media largely portrays teachers as good or bad rather than as whole, dynamic people. These negative images of teachers suggest that the public has not created a respected role for the teacher. Further, negative or limiting images of the teacher were found to bleed into teachers' self-perceptions, impacting their sense of empowerment and happiness. I mean, does that just make you want to sit down and cry, or what?

In the new era of the Common Core, I am perhaps most nervous that there will be no significant change for students. There was no pilot or incremental implementation that might give us insight as to whether *these* standards (as opposed to the standards that came before them) will yield positive gains for children. Is it possible that students will grow and progress in amazing ways? Of course it is. The Standards are the what—the goal we are trying to hit. As teachers, we have always been guided by a set of standards for each grade level. However, what makes me nervous is when the how—the methods that teachers will use to reach these standards—becomes tightly controlled. Call me crazy, but if these overly prescriptive hows fail to skyrocket children to the top of the charts, the fingers will be pointed squarely at the teachers—and the teachers alone.

The Silver Bullet

Speaking of overly prescriptive curricula, why is it that educational leaders (a.k.a. the outsiders) are still looking for the silver-bullet solution that will solve all of our educational and societal woes? It is a commonly held, but terribly flawed, assumption that programs or practices that are successful in one school can simply be replicated in any other school context (Darling-Hammond, 1997). Does it not seem crazy to think that there exists some magical one-size-fits-all solution in a box that will not only mitigate the effects of poverty but also have all children reading at or above grade level if you follow these 10 simple steps? The silver-bullet solution is like the Loch Ness Monster of the educational world. People claim to have seen it, but there's no tangible proof.

For years, I listened to my mother, a 41-year veteran of the classroom, talk about how if you waited long enough, every educational trend circles back around like high-waisted jeans. (Which, by the way, are largely a terrible idea. Much like educational trends, they do *not* work in every context.) Education is often dominated by trends. There is always some new finger-snapping way that we are going to get all kids to read (never mind getting them to actually *love* reading). These trends are usually based on some school or district where they have had success. Although many of these trends are well intentioned and well researched, it is impossible that they will yield the same results in every context. Yet, our obsession with finding the silver bullet means that teachers are often faced with a new philosophy, a new program, or a new curriculum each and every year. There never seems to be time for teachers to understand one method deeply or to take the time to master and tweak it over a period of several school years. Instead, many teachers feel as if the rug is continuously being pulled out from under them, that they are always behind in their understanding, and that they are not doing the best they can for their students.

Teachers are often lured into new reform programs only to find themselves doubly burdened by the expectations of their traditional roles and their new roles at the same time. Instead of making changes to teachers' fundamental practices, most reforms simply add on additional tasks and expectations (Cohen, 1995). In my own career, I can remember feeling excited about several curricular shifts. I remember thinking to myself more than once that perhaps *this* time, with *these* methods, we would better satisfy the needs of students. However, more often than not, at the end of the day, I found that there was more on my plate, not less. These popular new trends were often piled onto existing expectations; to-dos were added, and none were ever taken away.

In my mind, the silver bullet, if we must seek one out, should be shifting the paradigm so teachers are intimately involved in the creation of solutions to pressing educational issues. Rather than being the victim to the latest solution in a box, it is key that teachers are asked to study, practice, and discuss the latest educational trend to determine the potential lessons learned, monitoring and adjusting their work accordingly.

The Times Are Changing: Let's Change With Them!

Change in education is constant—and exhausting. Often, it feels like as soon as you've wrapped your head around the latest politically trendy shift, a finger-snapping idea on the part of some noneducator pulls the rug right out from underneath you. It often seems that as soon as we teachers begin to implement one shiny new mandate, another one is right behind it. Teachers are like contortionists that way; we are constantly bending and reshaping ourselves to align with the newest initiatives. Teachers are bombarded by change—change that seems to happen *to* us rather than *with* us.

> Ironically, "blaming" teachers for the failure of American education reinforce[s] the idea that teachers [can] be powerful agents in the education scene, able to make a difference by virtue of the decisions they ma[k]e on a day-to-day basis. (Cochran-Smith & Lytle, 1999, p. 16)

Too often, we appear to be victims of change rather than leading the charge and advocating for ourselves and our students. I say, "No more!" The reality is that change isn't going anywhere. And neither are we. So, I believe our only choice is to change our attitudes about change. We will be happier if we embrace the change instead of blindly digging in our heels and potentially missing out on an opportunity for professional growth. We can become a part of the change rather than a victim of it. We can look for the positive in the change rather than focus solely on the negative. We can choose to not let the change control us and make us miserable. We can initiate change rather than stand by and watch it happen to us.

Change is inevitable in our classrooms. To survive (and be deserving of that music video wind machine as we walk down the halls), we can no longer let changes get us down, or stray from what we know is best practice. Best practice is best practice, and we can no longer let mandates, off-the-wall assessments, and those who have never set foot in a classroom dictate how we run our classrooms. We can and should be agents of change. We can do this by carefully considering the changes that come our way, evaluating them for what they have to offer, and being open to learning new lessons about how to reach our students. We monitor and adjust thoughtfully rather than throwing the baby out with the bathwater.

Although our voices are not heard at the all-powerful decision-making table in significant ways, we can be confident in the knowledge we possess about our practice and the needs of our students in our particular context. Danielson (2007) writes that teachers are the keepers of the school culture and possess an institutional memory that is invaluable. We must own this reality and rise to the occasion by cultivating greater leadership roles within our school communities. In subsequent chapters, I discuss ways to take charge and to find your leadership potential. Start small, with a professional book club or a committee aimed at solving a small school issue. Increased teacher leadership is key to finding our happiness. It reduces teacher isolation while increasing the potential for varied responsibilities and expanded influence (Johnson & Donaldson, 2007). It is a first step toward getting a seat at the table.

I know, the demands are dizzying, and it is very easy to lose your way. It is also easy to fear for your job and your reputation if you don't conform. In these moments, I try to remind myself that my primary job is teach my little friends how to love reading, to make learning come alive, and to encourage them to follow and expand their interests. But, let this be the year that we take back control of our classrooms and define our practice for ourselves. If we want our students to be leaders, we have to be leaders ourselves. If we want our students to be fabulous, *we* have to be fabulous first.

CHAPTER 2

Let's Get Deep

Embrace Your Teaching Philosophy

> *I am who I am not yet.*
>
> —Maxine Greene (as quoted in Pinar, 1998, p. 1)

This tidbit has been so transformational for me that I need to share it with you. I want this written on a T-shirt or spray-painted on the wall of my classroom. It needs to at least be written on a tea bag label so I can see it from time to time and remind myself that even though I am working to my personal capacity (and beyond) most days, I am constantly on the road to becoming an improved version of myself: "I am who I am not yet." I am who I imagine myself to be on my best day. This thought keeps me sane and is like the North Star of my personal philosophy of what it means to be an educator.

Have you stopped to really think about the stereotypical images of "the teacher" that are popular in the media these days? Let me sum them up for you. Image 1 is a disheveled mess who is so lazy that it's a miracle that she gets to work every day. She is unconcerned with the needs of her students because she is too busy planning for "all that time off" in the summer and making shopping lists so that when she runs out the school's door at 3:00 p.m. on the dot with absolutely no work to do at home, she is prepared to do nothing related to the classroom. She drinks coffee continually and spends most of the school day sitting passively at her desk, giving out worksheets. These are the teachers often found by the news media. They are interviewed or mocked and held up as an example that represents all of us. OK, reality check. Does this teacher exist? Yes. I have actually worked with this type of teacher (I use the term *work* loosely). Is she the norm? No.

Let's take a look at image 2. The other teacher—made popular by various movies, books, and made-for-television minidramas—literally does nothing but teach, plan, make meals for the homeless, and then teach some more while rescuing a litter of puppies. Not that there is anything wrong with any of those things, but *come on*. This teacher is either dressed head to toe in leather (badass but impractical) or content to live in the same three outfits in a teeny apartment because who cares about how comfortable your home is when you spend *every* waking hour at school? Does this teacher exist? Yes. Is she the norm? No.

Although these two images of "the teacher" are common, there are about a million other stereotypes and boatloads of misinformation floating around out there about what it means to be a teacher. And while I completely support you in shooting dirty looks at people who make comments such as, "It must be nice to have summers off," I beg you not to fall victim to these stereotypes. Don't fall down the rabbit hole! The ways in which teachers are portrayed in popular media shape the stereotypes that the general public holds about us. In turn, these stereotypes live on to have a negative impact on the formation of new teachers' sense of self in the classroom (Weber & Mitchell, 1995). So, not only are these stereotypes leading to inane comments about our summer breaks, but they are also playing a part in how we think about ourselves as professionals. Am I the only one who finds this disturbing? We must stand strong in our vision of teaching and what it means to be a teacher who is deserving of a music video wind machine and a superhero cape for general fabulousness.

My own thoughts about who I want to become and the beliefs I hold sacred as a teacher have grown out of a million stories that are particular to my experience. In this chapter, I want to outline my philosophy of teaching for you and put out into the world who I am not yet but am on the road to becoming. I am not sharing this with you because I think it is the one and only way to be. I am sharing this because I want you to think about and question your own philosophy of teaching. This might be something that you haven't had the time or luxury (or desire) to do since your days in Education 101, but these ideas and ideals can and should be the basis of your decision making within your practice. We can no longer allow fear and people who have never set foot in a classroom to drive our decision making. If we lose track of who we are as teachers and what we believe in, then they win and we lose. We lose our sense of joy as teachers, we lose our ability to be as effective as possible, and perhaps most tragic, we begin to lose our authentic connection to our little friends.

As you read this chapter and the details of my personal teaching philosophy, take some time to consider your own teaching philosophy. Remember, your philosophy of teaching will be unique and reflective of your own experiences in school and your ideals for yourself as an educator, so I want you to use my thoughts as a springboard. Do you agree with my ideas? Do you disagree? What thoughts guide your conception of what it means to be a teacher? Who do you want to be that you are not yet? And how can you go about becoming that kind of teacher? Per the wise words of Maxine Greene, who are you on the road to becoming?

My Philosophy: Classrooms Should Be Spaces Characterized by Caring Relationships

I strive to create a classroom learning environment that is characterized by an ethic of caring (Noddings, 1988/1994). By prioritizing the relationship between myself and my little friends, I push myself to find and develop ways to know them deeply both as people and as learners. It is too tempting (and too prevalent a practice) to label students with broad terms such as *high achieving* or *behavioral problem* and to allow our conversations about students to be dominated by academics, shortcomings, and test scores. However, we do not work in a factory and are not turning out widgets that must all fit into the same hole. Our students are growing individuals, and we, as their teachers, are literally growing the minds of our future generation. Yes, it may sound like some "Wind Beneath My Wings" type of theme song should be playing in the background when I say that, and you should feel free to mock me. But you know I'm right. This overall goal of mine to

> Once we know who we are and what we're about in the classroom, we become intentional in our teaching; we do what we do *on purpose*, with good reason. Intentional teachers are thoughtful, reflective people who are conscious of the decisions they make and the actions they take; they live and teach by the principles and practices they value and believe in. (Miller, 2008, p. 4)

develop successful and caring relationships with my students guides my decisions about my teaching practices in a number of ways.

Knowing Your Students as People

Sometimes it may be easy to lose track of why you got into teaching, but I can bet that one of the many reasons you pursued this profession was because you enjoy spending time with children and are aware of how much joy teaching can bring. Yes, joy. Remember that? It is highly related to fun and should be something that is a constant in your classroom.

Sadly, I know this is often easier said than done. I remember one November when I was deep in the weeds of report card time. Report card time should come with its own ominous music and prescription medication. There is data, more data, some progress monitoring, and then even more data, which means piles, piles, and more piles of information. I had become obsessed with my to-do list, and in a frantic effort to check everything off my list and just get it all done without having a complete meltdown, I became a blur of efficiency. I had just sat down to eat lunch (read: cram lukewarm leftovers from last night into my mouth in 10 minutes or less so I can get back to checking things off the aforementioned list) when my colleague sighed and said, "We are lucky to have a job that is so much fun." Because I'm all class, I responded by practically choking myself midsnort before it occurred to me that I used to think my job was fun, too. My students are fun. We have *fun* together. Learning is fun. I then spent the remainder of my lunch sharing silly stories from my classroom with my colleague, and we had a good laugh. And then, before all of that goodness and joy was sucked from my being by the piles lurking on every available surface of my classroom, I took the time to think about each and every one of my students to remember times when I had observed them being funny, kind, or inspired. I jotted down these stories and tucked them away for conference night.

That year (and *every* year since), I prided myself on being an expert kid watcher, charged with finding the stories that make teaching worthwhile and highlight the joy that's there when you look close enough. I now begin all of my parent conferences with a quick story about the child as an individual—not the data producer, the *child*. These stories remind me of the joy and, at the same time, frame my conversations with parents by starting from a place of connection and fun—because school is fun.

I just went all mushy on you, right? But it's true, I love my little friends. Granted, I may have to push myself to find something I love about each and *every* little friend, but I do because the idea of connecting to my students in meaningful ways is paramount to maintaining the fun and joy in my teaching in so many ways. Anything that compromises my ability to connect with them and nurture a reciprocal relationship is something I refuse to do.

Knowing Your Students as Learners and Readers

The teaching of reading is not just about dispensing and practicing a variety of grade-level–appropriate skills and strategies. Although those skills and strategies certainly help and give students the tools to move forward, they are not enough. Our primary and most important job is to teach children a love for reading and its many purposes.

Let's be real: The climate of many of our schools today is all about data, benchmarks, and dividing students into leveled groups that are then labeled by color, much like our national security levels. Red means we must collect more data and implement a host of strategies! Yellow means we must progress monitor! It is easy to get caught up in these systems and charts and graphs (oh my!). But what about the learners who are trapped under all of that data? What do we know about our students as readers?

One of my favorite types of conferences to have with students is more like an interview in which my primary goal is to uncover that student's reading identity. I consciously and continually share tidbits of my reading life with my students. They see the magazines poking out of my workbag. They watch me take books out of our school library. They know about my obsession with digital home decorating magazines and blogs. I take care to share my reading life with my students in an effort to be as authentic as possible in my teaching (Miller, 2014). So, I make it a priority to know about their loves when it comes to reading. What genres make them excited to read? What text types do they like best? Why do they read? How many authors can they name, and which ones do they prefer? What are they interested in knowing more about? Not only does this information help me keep my library stocked with high-interest texts, but it also helps me slowly push my students beyond their current reading to try new authors, genres, or text types: "Sweetheart, I know you love to read fantasy, so I was thinking you might be interested in this informational article about the history of a few famous castles. Think it's worth a read?" And honestly, I don't really care if students are reading a take-out menu, as long as they are jazzed about reading and are reading with purpose.

I have seen my fair share of reluctant readers—the little friends who struggle to select a book, stick with a book, or feel excited about their reading. One little guy in particular stands out in my mind because he worked so hard to cover up his reading struggles. Every day he would diligently take out his independent reading selections and dutifully pretend to read them. Seriously, this kid could have won a Tony for his performance. I caught on after a day or so and made my way over to confer with him about my observations. When I asked him why he was working so hard to pretend to read his books, he explained that it wasn't necessarily that the books were too hard for him but that he just didn't love any of them. He said he felt "just OK" about books but knew how much I loved them and was worried about hurting my feelings, so each day he pretended. (Does it get any sweeter?) A few days later, we were on the playground when I noticed my little guy stooped over a crack in the blacktop. He was consumed with watching a group of ants while soccer, tag, and general screaming swirled around him. "Do you like ants?" I asked. "Like them?" he replied, "I love them! I always look for anthills on the sidewalk outside my building and make sure no one steps on them." Suddenly, I recalled our conversation about reading; it was like the stars had aligned in my favor. "Sweetheart, did you know there are books about ants?" "There are?" he asked, wide-eyed. "You mean whole books? Books all about ants?" "There are," I answered. "Why don't we take a walk to the library?" Together we found several books on ants to get him started, and my little friend was hooked. He read every book under the sun about ants—sometimes engaging with text that was far too easy and instead spending days poring over the photographs, while other times he pushed himself to work with more challenging texts, motivated by the promise of learning something new about his beloved insects. Now, I don't know if my friend is an avid reader today, but I know that he is aware that there *are* books for him and that if he puts in some effort, he is a reader, not a pretender.

Working Collaboratively With Students

A key piece to my approach to teaching is finding appropriate places to involve my students in the creation of the classroom, from the physical environment to our routines. One thing I have learned about most teachers and myself over the years is that we are inherently control freaks. We like to make a plan for everything, from the order of the colors used on anchor charts (rainbow order only!) to the type of pen we use to take conference notes (fine point, of course!). We like systems and order and routines because they are a beautiful thing. However, part of establishing a caring relationship with your students means relinquishing some control and sharing it with them. Caring is sharing. Yes, you can still use your favorite pen and obsess over your system for filing, but you might want to think about places where you can embrace a more collaborative setup.

I can almost see you raising an eyebrow as you think to yourself, This all sounds good, but exactly what does she mean? What sort of decisions am I involving the class in? You might want to start with some collaborative goal setting, such as how many books you're going to read as a class over the next week or month. Of course, we can't let our students go rogue and set a ridiculous goal such as 1,543 books next week, but we can guide them gently toward setting an appropriate and realistic goal. I also allow my students the chance to select the class read-aloud from time to time or to vote on an upcoming author study, honoring the importance of their voice as readers and as members of a reading community (Miller, 2009).

The importance of this practice came to me as I stomped around my classroom at the end of a school day, fuming about how, in their decision making, the administration never seemed to consider what teachers wanted. As I drafted a scathing e-mail in my mind (which is usually where they stay), I realized that although I should find an appropriate way to voice my concern, it was likely that my e-mail alone was not going to change much. And I hated having no control. (Again, the control freak emerges.) Then, I realized how hypocritical it was for me to be upset about not having a voice in larger school decision making when I was not making regular opportunities for my students to have a voice in classroom decision making. Why should I be the only one who decides what gets read aloud or who gets to partner with whom? From that day forward, I found appropriate ways to involve my class in meaningful decisions that impacted our day. By modeling what I wanted the larger school environment to look and feel like,

I not only felt more empowered within but also allowed my students to feel empowered in their learning.

Holding Students Accountable

Did you just shudder when you read the word *accountable*? I think I might have just gagged even as I typed it, but it really is kind of important. In a classroom characterized by caring relationships between the teacher and students, the active participation and responsiveness of both parties is essential (Noddings, 1988/1994). Translation? Your students meet you halfway by trying suggested strategies, sharing their struggles honestly, and setting goals for their own work. In turn, you respond to their needs clearly, quickly, and patiently. Doesn't that sound fabulous? Well, it is fabulous and possible.

I first began to embrace this philosophy one year when reading conferences had been humming along in my room. The routine and logistics of it all were fine, but I felt like I was walking uphill in molasses in January, as my grandmother would say. Every week I felt like I met with students to deliver the same conference that I had had with them the week prior. Yet, for some reason, I dutifully took my conference notes, redid the conference, and moved on. Then, one day—probably a day when coffee was scarce and therefore impatience was running high—I became especially frustrated with the kids' lack of progress. That's when I realized that I had become comfortable repeating the same learning over and over and over without expecting any buy-in or effort on the part of my students. Why would I expect them to do anything other than sit and politely humor me? Why weren't any of them trying the strategies that we had discussed and practiced together? I mean, every time someone got stuck on a word, the kid looked to me, rather than within, to solve it. One day, I had to stop myself before screaming, "Just look at the list of strategies we've gone over a million times! It's right there on the wall!" That was the moment when I knew I had to think of ways to place more responsibility on my students to at least try some of the fabulousness I had bestowed on them. Plus, when I thought about it, the idea of *not* expecting them to try what we had discussed seemed almost disrespectful on some level. It was as if I was somehow sending them a message that I didn't think they could do it without me.

In my own practice, I have found that leaving behind some sort of artifact of my teaching during small-group or one-on-one time helps students take ownership of their learning and feel a sense of responsibility to engage in the learning process independently. By an artifact, I mean something little and quick to make that will trigger their memories and help them work on a given skill or toward a specific goal independently as well as with my support. Does this mean I transfer total responsibility to the students and never check in with them on it again? Definitely not. It means that my students are comfortable with this practice and see these "leave-behinds" as gentle reminders as to what their focus should be when reading independently. I like to think that they look at these artifacts and think, Oh right. Mrs. Scoggin, my amazing and totally fabulous teacher, wants me to work on this idea that we discussed yesterday, so I'll get right on top of that. And, wow, her hair looks great today! (Or, you know, something along those lines.)

I use a variety of organizational items as artifacts. Sometimes I jot down on a sticky note a goal we discussed that can be inserted into any text or simply left on the student's desk as a reminder. Other times, I use an index card when I want to bullet-point several ideas or strategies for the student to attempt. I have also been known to grab a half sheet of fancy paper, some fluorescent cardstock, or a homemade bookmark made from construction paper. Basically, I carry around with me a "tool kit" (read: plastic zip bag) that contains all of these items so I can grab whatever strikes me without getting up, running to my desk, and breaking the precious connection (read: teaching juju) that I have created with the student during our time together.

Let me give you an example of how I might integrate one of these artifacts into my conferring work. When I work with a student who is struggling to independently call on a set of strategies (e.g., for decoding a tricky word, uncovering the theme of a text, or discovering the meaning of an unfamiliar word), I take out my trusty index card and do a quick assessment. I begin by asking the student to name the strategies that he or she might use to tackle the desired goal. As the student shares his or her thinking with me, we work together to quickly create a mini–strategy chart. This chart helps me understand what strategies that student is comfortable with and the strategies that are still out of reach. I do some quick coaching into how the student might use the strategy chart independently and then leave him or her to it.

Moving forward, I focus my upcoming conferring work on those strategies that the student did *not* name, adding to the chart as we go. By leaving behind a mini–strategy chart, I've provided a concrete artifact of my teaching and a clue as to what that student should be working on as an independent reader. After all, it doesn't really matter if the student can figure out the meaning of a new word with me sitting right there; it matters whether my little friend can do it when no one else is holding his or her hand.

Rethinking the Use of Time During the School Day

One thing that continually interferes with my achievement of philosophical Zen in my classroom is time—as in there is never enough! Believe me, I wholeheartedly support the arts, but if I have to coordinate my conferring schedule with one more trumpet lesson or assembly rehearsal, I think I may just run screaming down the hallway in a fit of frustration (just being honest). And although I definitely support advocating for an uninterrupted block of classroom time within which to dispel your genius regarding reading and to allow your students to fall into their books, I am also a realist, so I know that change of this nature is often beyond slow. So, what often happens is that I begin to feel as if I am cramming a tremendous amount of instruction into an ever-shrinking amount of time, and when that happens, my teaching takes on a frantic pace. This frantic feeling most definitely translates to my little friends and begins to create an atmosphere that is not conducive to falling in love with reading or allowing students the space to challenge themselves. Essential to creating a classroom characterized by an ethic of caring (Noddings, 1988/1994) is the use of time to privilege the deepening of your relationships with students rather than falling victim to an obsession with completing tasks on a set schedule.

So, how do we find a moment to take a breath and regain the sense of calm and purposefulness we want to embody? For me, taking a breath meant spending the first three to five minutes of my students' independent reading time with my own book. Yes, you read that correctly. I sent my students back to their seats to read and then picked up my own book and read for a few minutes while they settled into their own reading.

Clearly, the text they saw me read was very intentional—occasionally a chapter book by one of my favorite authors, sometimes an article from the newspaper, a digital text, or a class favorite. I used this time to not only model good reading behaviors but also to reinforce for students my own love of reading. Believe me when I tell you that those three to five minutes of reading on my own were transformational. They allowed me to take a breath. They allowed me to focus my thoughts. They allowed me to feel in control of our time and demonstrate for students what I wanted them to do as readers. Give it a try for just two weeks and see if it makes a difference, because doing nothing but complaining isn't going to fix anything.

After years of feeling frustrated with my lack of control over how time was used during the school day, I also decided to take back some control by manipulating the time I did have control over. Granted, I wasn't left with a tremendous amount, but even reframing how I used lunch every once in a while felt liberating. I know teachers' "free" time during the day is limited. I use the word *free* liberally here because I know that not even lunch is sacred and that the concept of free time is laughable. Most of us choke down some leftovers and then dash off to make copies, go to the bathroom, set up for math, check our mail, return some e-mails, and generally run around like whirlwinds of productivity. So, I'm not talking about rethinking each and every lunch time, rather just one or two a month. Shall we snuggle up for a quick story?

One year I had a super special friend in my class who was sweet, shy, and very smart. He was not the most popular kid in my class and often had trouble relating to everyone. He once told me that his life's ambition was to be (and I quote) a "vegetarian bus driver," so from here on out, we'll just call him the Bus Driver. The Bus Driver desperately needed to be held up as a trendsetter and to be celebrated for all he had to offer. He also needed some quality time with an adult to nurture his insane love of reading. Every day I felt frustrated that my time was not my own and that I was unable to spend uninterrupted time with the Bus Driver, discussing and sharing our insights on books, so I took control of the time that was my own and invited him to have a private book club with me at lunchtime. The plan was to chat about books together over our lunches and then send him on his way to recess if he chose to go. The Bus Driver was fairly nonchalant when he replied, "Sure," and sauntered out the door at dismissal. "Oh well," I thought to myself, "here goes nothing."

The next day, he showed up in a full suit: a jacket, a tie, a button-down shirt, and pressed pants. Keep in mind that I did not teach in a wealthy school district—quite the opposite, in fact. This outfit represented some serious effort. My first thought upon seeing him that morning was, Oh no! Did I forget about Picture Day?! My second thought was, Ugh, I am so not wearing what I wanted to wear in the class picture. And my third thought was, Wait, a suit? What's going on here? So, I asked him, "Sweetheart, you look so handsome! Did I forget Picture Day? Why are you so dressed up?" He replied, "For our book club date today, of course. It's a special day!"

Are you dying from a heart overflowing with love for the Bus Driver now?

That day, I put my usual gossip session and frantic classroom errands on hold to enjoy a book club lunch date with the Bus Driver, and it was amazing. I felt my panic about time melt away and was absorbed by our conversation and the feeling that I was doing something that was truly right for my student. We began to meet every other week, and soon other kids were asking to join to see what it was all about. The Bus Driver became known as the go-to guy for a good book recommendation and as someone who was to be respected for his ability to read. As a teacher, this is how I want to be able to use my time. Rather than sit and wait for someone to provide me with the perfect opportunity, I made my own opportunity and, at the same time, created a ritual that made me feel like I was on the road to becoming the type of teacher I truly want to be. Who can't be happy about that?

My Philosophy: Classrooms Should Be Places Where Anything Is Possible and Independent Choice Empowers

Another key piece about my practice is maintaining my classroom as a place where students are free to imagine what might be possible for themselves, their community, and the world. Even as I typed that, I recognized that it might sound a bit like an answer that a contestant might give during a Miss America pageant when asked how she might change the climate of education in our country. (At this point, we might as well ask pageant contestants because we basically have allowed everyone but actual teachers to share what they think is a good idea.) But I'm serious about this one. In my very nerdy doctoral days, I sat in the living room of a brilliant educator and let her thoughts about what learning should feel like wash over me, hoping something would stick. One of her most intriguing ideas was that of developing a social imagination (Greene, 1998) in children, fostering their ability to actively question the world around them and ask questions such as, "What ought to be?" and "What can we do to get there?" I mean, does that sound fabulous or what? Don't you want to be in that classroom?

From that moment forward, I filtered each new initiative, curriculum, and lesson plan through this lens by considering how I could use it or tweak it to maintain that sense of possibility. I flexed my own social imagination to consider what ought to be, and instead of stopping there as my vision went up in flames of impossibility, I pushed myself to think about what I could do in my classroom to take small steps toward actually getting there. In terms of my reading instruction specifically, it meant a fierce dedication to the notion of student choice of reading material and creating spaces to talk about texts deeply.

As I do so often in my practice, I began by reflecting on my own reading life to realize the importance and power of having choice in reading material. Choice is critical in fostering a love of reading in students (Allington, 2012; Miller, 2009). As a reader, I can go weeks without reading an actual book, instead losing myself in mindless magazines (*People* magazine, I heart you endlessly), home decorating blogs (oh, what I could do with some sandpaper and paint), and links to articles on Facebook (yes, I admit it.) Then, one night I'll pick up a book from the permanent stack on my nightstand and dive in headfirst. If that is what my *real* reading life looks like—not my reading life as it has been tested by endless Scantron sheets— then that is what it should look like in my classroom. I can take small steps toward this by allowing my students to have the same freedom of choice in text type, genre, and subject matter.

As I began to find space to take these small steps in my own practice, I felt empowered and wanted to create ways for this sense of possibility to permeate the way my students and I interacted with one another. But I knew that I had to cultivate a climate in which all of my students felt safe sharing before I could push them to develop their own sense of social imagination. I know this sounds obvious, but when we are talking about something as personal and potentially difficult as learning how to read, which isn't easy for everyone, making it OK for students to share their private thoughts and struggles with the class becomes more of a challenge.

My biggest concern wasn't the little friends who presented obvious behavioral issues because they were the focus of my time and energy so often; it was my quiet, well-behaved, happy-to-fly-under-the-radar friends, those who often have the most interesting and intriguing reactions to text, whom I worried about the most. Suddenly, classic classroom rules such as "Don't talk while others are talking" and "Don't laugh at the answers your friends give" began to feel negative. So much limitation and not enough possibility. So, I reframed my conversation about classroom rules by talking to students about what might be possible if we all respect and listen to one another. We held several conversations focused on the questions "What ought to be in our classroom?" and "How can we take small steps to get there?" This shift definitely worked to make me feel more positive and as if I were promoting the idea of possibility within the classroom, but I had no idea if these concepts had truly been absorbed by my little friends. And then something happened.

The entire class was sitting in the library on the rug with their self-selected independent book choices. Each student had chosen a text with a character who encountered a problem that resonated with the reader in some way, and the students had all brought their texts and the classroom rug to the library in preparation to share their thoughts with a partner. I knew that the lesson might be sensitive and that there would be students who would be reluctant to share, but I went for it anyway: "Remember, if you really feel uncomfortable sharing, you can just pass and listen to your partner." On my cue, partners dutifully turned and began to chat with their partners. As I bopped around the rug to listen in on conversations, I overheard one particularly confident little friend attempt to coax a more shy student to share his thoughts: "Come on, I really want to hear your thinking," he said. Nothing. "I bet you have really interesting ideas," he tried again. Nothing. A nearby student who also heard the exchange chimed in: "Yeah, we want to hear what you think, too. You don't share that often, but I bet you have good ideas." My shy friend looked uncertain as a growing number of students became aware of what was going on. Another student offered, "It's not as bad as you think it is in your mind. It will be OK." Suddenly, a majority of the class was focused on my shy friend, and I worried that he might actually burst into tears. But then he stood and walked to the front of the rug. A round of encouraging applause spontaneously broke out around the rug, and my shy friend straightened up and shared his thinking. Everyone listened, and then they all clapped, and a few students offered compliments. A slow smile spread across my shy friend's face. In that moment, I knew that imagining possibilities would be embraced in my class, and this is an ideal that I will keep striving for, no matter what trendy political mandate comes my way.

My Philosophy: Teachers Should Model and Embrace Critically Reflective Practices

We get better at doing something by reflecting critically on our current performance and thinking specifically about how we can improve. This holds true for everything, whether you're learning how to juggle or working to become a better and more effective teacher. (Although, honestly, it can sometimes be difficult to tell the difference between a juggler and a teacher, but that's another story for another day.) While I admit that I spent a lot of time tooting my own horn and fantasizing about having my own theme music, something I don't often show people (and I probably should) is that I am incredibly hard on myself and end most of my days by lying in bed and thinking, What could I have done better today? Sometimes the answer is about being more patient with my glorious 3-year-old girl, and other times the answer is about a line of questioning that I should have pursued in a read-aloud.

Each time I teach a lesson, dust off a tried-and-true reading unit of study, or pull out a favorite read-aloud, I try to take a moment to reflect: How effective was this when I used it last year? Was there anything I wanted to change? Should I take a new approach with this particular class? Is there a better, more fresh way to approach this? (That last one is my personal favorite.) Don't worry, I'm not advocating that we throw the baby out with the bathwater every time there's a new trend in reading instruction. However, what I *am* advocating for is thinking critically about past practices to determine whether they are, in fact, still the best path to take. If I find myself thinking, Well, I've always done it that way, so it must be OK, it's like a red flag because that answer is rarely good enough.

Classroom practices are a heavily researched area, and if there is a better, newer, fresher way of approaching a classic instructional strategy, I want to know about it. Doing something because you've always done it a certain way can be troubling because students and research on best practice are constantly evolving. Let me put it this way: Would you rather have your appendix removed by the surgeon who stays current with the research and therefore will conduct your surgery laparoscopically or by the surgeon who hasn't given any serious thought to current research and therefore would like to cut you from stem to stern when removing your organ? Uh, yeah, I thought so. Why should it be any different for teachers? We definitely want to stay fresh and on our game because it ups the level of engagement for everyone.

Related to staying fresh with our practices, here's a riddle for you: What single word has the power to strike fear in the hearts of many teachers while at the same time thrilling others? You guessed it! Technology. I'll pause for you to roll your eyes, squeal with excitement, or sigh. Friends, it's here. For those of you who may snub the current research on the Internet or social media, I hate to be the one to break it to you, but it's not going anywhere. Plus, kids dig it and are using it anyway, so isn't it our responsibility to harness the power of the screen and use it for good, not evil?

Here's a quick example of how a simple technological tweak had a class full of fifth graders jazzed about crafting written summaries of their reading. I think we can all agree that writing a summary of our reading is right up there with clipping your toenails or scrubbing a toilet. Translation? It's not exciting, but it's a necessary skill. As a general rule, I like to make my instruction something that doesn't result in rampant eye rolling or general malaise. I also try to make the writing that I ask students to do during their reading time to be purposeful and important (because our little friends should be reading during reading time). But as I reflected critically on my own practice, I realized that for years, summary writing had been a task I simply assigned to my students with the attitude that we just needed to do it to show that we can and then move on to something more interesting. In other words, no one was really happy.

So, when it came time to again ask my little friends to write summaries of their reading, we headed to Twitter. The format of a tweet (which limits the author to 140 characters) already forces students to keep their writing tight and to seriously consider their word choice. However, jazzing up summary writing through the creation of tweets that only I would read and critique was not enough; I wanted a greater purpose for their work. Therefore, instead, we discussed using the summaries as teasers for the class to use when considering their future reading selections. By adding a common hashtag to easily view their work collectively, we had instantly created a meaningful reason for students to write summaries in a dynamic format that piqued their interest. To that, I say game, set, match. You can't help but feel happy when you develop a successful new lesson that highly engages your little friends in meaningful work.

I know that many of you are working in classrooms with three dusty desktops from 1993, only two of which work well and maybe even rely on the alignment of the moon to establish a decent Wi-Fi connection. Smoke signals may occasionally feel faster than the speed of the Internet you have available. I hear you. My advice to you is to work with whatever technology you have available. Sign up for the computer lab every day or monopolize the rolling cart of laptops—whatever you have to do to establish the need for more technology to your administration. Methinks just talking about it in irritated tones is no longer enough, and by the by, it is probably bringing you down. Doing something constructive about a problem such as this is often much more rewarding than complaining—and this is coming from a lover of complaining.

I also know that many of you reading this may be unsure of how to implement technology meaningfully or are afraid of not having everything go perfectly when you include it in a lesson. I get it. It's hard to feel fabulous when it seems like the ship is sinking around you. So, let's reframe how we think about struggling with the implementation of something new, such as technology. What do we expect from our students when we present them with a challenge? I expect a significant amount of effort. I also expect students to remain positive when they encounter trouble spots and, rather than give up, to be problem solvers. When we consider the implementation of technology in our classrooms from this angle, it seems to present an opportunity to model these behaviors in front of and in collaboration with our students. It presents us with the opportunity to tap into their expertise (they soak up technology like sponges!) and let them help us so we can also model that asking for and receiving help is nothing to be ashamed of.

In a nutshell, reflecting on my own practice has been key to my own professional growth. Questions swirled in my head almost every night as

I lay in bed: What am I doing well? What about my day could have gone better? What am I afraid to try in my classroom, and why? What new methods or strategies sound intriguing for incorporating into my practice? However, while the constant questioning sometimes kept me up at night, it also pushed me to see my teaching practice as something organic and ever evolving.

My Philosophy: Emphasize the Joy of Reading and Learning

I am not sure why I got into teaching, but I think that deep in our bones, we teachers know it is something that we're supposed to do. Some of us know very early, and others are called to teaching after years in another, less fulfilling career. After I got over my dreams of being a cosmetologist (seriously), I knew I wanted to be a teacher. My oldest friend and I would spend snowy Sundays taping ourselves (on an actual cassette tape…I am so old) reading books aloud. We partner read the books, complete with voices for each of the characters and sound effects. It was equal parts amazing and intensely dorky. A few months ago, I dug out my old Walkman (clearly, I need to do some purging) and listened to our old performances. Although I was horrified by how I sound on tape, I was overwhelmed by the joy and love of reading that came through loud and clear. We loved reading, and now, a few decades later, we are both avid, active lovers of reading.

I was fortunate enough to grow up in a house full of readers. My grandmother read the newspaper each and every day, and I can still picture her with a smudge of newsprint on her cheek. My stepfather was always working through a book about the *Titanic* or a paperback with a helicopter or boat on the front. My mother dedicated her summers to reading the Nutmeg Book Award winners and always had a stack of novels on her nightstand. She and I routinely went to the library, where I would fill a bag with books for myself and then delight in the excitement of wandering through the impressive stacks of grown-up books as she browsed for herself. As adults, we constantly talk about, recommend, and exchange books, although I can't quite meet her penchant for historical fiction and biographies. I have a clear sense of who I am as a reader—what I like, what I read to challenge myself, what I read when I want to decompress, what

I want to read next, and what I think I ought to tackle someday. I pick up each new text with purpose: Tonight I'll read to learn, tonight I'll read to enjoy, tonight I'll read to try to better myself, tonight I'll read to try and figure out why my youngest child won't just take a nap already! Through reading, I have experienced other people's adventures, learned about their conflicts, and lived a million lifetimes.

Not every child is fortunate enough to be raised in a house dominated by a love of reading. I knew that many of my students lived in households with few texts and were not routinely exposed to what it looks like to have an active reading life. It is imperative that we prioritize the joy of reading, pushing children to see beyond the strategies and skills and into the possibilities created by texts. We don't want to simply create proficient readers; we want to cultivate avid, voracious readers who have full and active reading lives (Miller, 2014). This begins by careful consideration of the texts you share with your students through read-alouds, book previews, close readings, personal recommendations, and small-group discussions. Are you including an adequate range of text types, genres, and authors so each reader can see some aspect of his or her identity reflected in your choices? Are you exposing students to a wide variety of possibilities for expansion of their reading preferences? If you find that you come up with the same types of go-to texts, embrace the challenge of finding fresh read-alouds.

It wasn't until I mapped out my key read-alouds across a calendar that I was able to see the patterns in my own choices and find the space for change. Once I recognized where I needed to alter my text selections, I reverted back to that deeply nerdy girl who read aloud into a cassette tape. I have always found the discovery of another wonderful book to be thrilling, and for me, reading children's literature has always been so much more than simply another task on my to-do list. Rather, it has always felt like a privilege that this was actually part of my job.

Beyond the choice of books we share with our students, it is important to consider *how* we share them as well. I have watched many a painful read-aloud that is so void of joy that I felt like yelling, "Fire!" just to help those students escape. Granted, I have a flair for the dramatic (who knew?), so making a read-aloud into a performance is something I enjoy. I know this isn't for everyone. I'm not talking about using a variety of accents (although I do a mean Strega Nona) or dramatic facial expressions. I am talking about the passion and enthusiasm you exude as you share a book, your thoughts about that book, and the strategies you might try to further unlock the deeper meaning of the text with your friends. What I am trying to say is that explicit instruction in reading should not mean the death of all things joyful. Too many times, I have heard teachers claim that there are so many strategies and skills and standards to cover that there's no time left over to enjoy the book. But why does sharing a strategy or thinking aloud in pursuit of reaching a particular standard mean that there's no joy? I get that standards in and of themselves are not filled with joyful music, but they're standards, not a marching band. The joy comes from us. It is our duty to present these ideas, these skills, and these texts with a sense of joy, appreciation, and enthusiasm. It's all in the presentation!

Letting Your Philosophy Be Your Guide

Thinking through your personal philosophy of education may seem very reminiscent of Education 101. After all, your existing to-do list is most likely also spawning more baby to-do lists, and it may already seem like there's no possible way that you can keep up with it all. I get it. I've been there. I have run to the photocopier, stopped at the bathroom, returned an e-mail to a parent, put up a bulletin board, and had a cup of coffee in 10 minutes flat. Teaching can feel like running a race—uphill. Yet, I would bet that a lot of your running and assorted other busy-ness is related to the unceasing changes that plague education: changes in curriculum, changes in leadership, changes in standards, changes in assessment and evaluation practices. Change isn't going anywhere, and it is easy to get lost in the minutiae and forget about the teacher you are or the teacher you want to become. To help you revise how you will approach all of this change, take back control of your professional life and happiness by using your philosophical beliefs about what it means to be an effective teacher or what it means to create a dynamic school experience for students. A wise mentor of mine once advised me that teaching is inherently filled with highs and lows and that it becomes our jobs as teachers to ride those waves and find some balanced, even ground. I have yet to find a true balance or fully become the teacher I envision myself to be. However, I have found a sense of happiness (and far fewer lows) when I allow these thoughts to guide my choices.

CHAPTER 3

Let's Get Physical

Creating Classroom Environments That Promote Reading, Independence for Students, and Personal Zen for You

I needed to change the lens through which I viewed everything familiar.

—Gretchen Rubin (2011, p. 3)

can't think of many spaces more familiar than our own classrooms. Although they are a familiar home away from home, they often get overlooked outside of those first few days before the kiddos arrive. We put things in places because "they have always been there," often with little consideration of an alternative. We pile because there seems to be a never-ending stream of things to pile. However, the organization of our physical space has a profound effect on our spiritual happiness. I felt like such a hippie writing that last sentence, but it's true, right? Do a quick Google search on the negative impact of disorganization and clutter, and you will find that an astonishing number of people are thinking and talking about how physical clutter and a lack of the routines that bring order to our lives can drastically impact our sense of well-being, happiness, and even ability to make decisions. (Cut to me saying, "I told you so.")

In a study on the impact of classroom organization on kindergarten students' learning motivation, it was found that raising the level of organization observed in a classroom correlated with a higher level of learning motivation in children. More specifically, it was revealed that quality classroom organization allowed teachers to take a proactive rather than reactive approach to discipline; to establish clear, stable routines; and to carefully monitor student progress and engagement in classroom work (Pakarinen et al., 2010). Translation? Creating an organized classroom space characterized by strong routines can actually contribute to making us better teachers. It increases the potential for us to nip behavioral issues in the bud, spend more time interacting with our students, and address their individual needs. I don't know about you, but classroom organization and the establishment of clear routines sounds like the first step in educational utopia. Tell me the truth: Can you feel the joy yet?

As teachers, it may feel as if there are many things beyond our control that drastically impact our days and have the potential to bring us down. However, one essential piece that we can lay claim to is the organization and ambience of our classrooms. Yes, I did just use the word *ambience* to describe a classroom: Everything from the colors we choose for bulletin boards to what we choose to post on our walls to the personal touches that reflect our own personalities and interests all add up to some serious classroom ambience. I don't know about you, but walking into my classroom when it is organized, ready for the day, and filled with beautiful examples of student work makes me feel happy. It makes me feel calm, on top of my game, and ready for the day. When I walk into my classroom on those other days—you know, those days when piles lurk in *every* corner and on any available surface, labels are missing from baskets, pencils lay strewn about without a proper home, and (gasp) books can be found lying in dusty corners—I feel sad, overwhelmed, and like I am behind even before the day begins. Just conjuring up that image makes me feel bad about myself. Where is the joy in that?

My classroom is my kingdom. It is my home away from home; it is one of the places I feel most like myself and is the backdrop for doing what I love (most days). I take the ritual of setting up my classroom each year very seriously. As in, there are to-do lists, hand-drawn maps, and organizational projects as far as the eye can see. As a self-proclaimed organizational goddess, I firmly believe that an organized classroom is a happy classroom. Students aside, I find happiness and inner Zen in those moments when I systematically work my way around the edges of my classroom, putting everything back where it belongs and setting up the various systems that help my classroom hum with productivity. When you are able to quickly locate that paper that no one else on your grade-level team can seem to find, doesn't that make you feel like a total rock star? Come on, own your inner organizationally nerdy tendencies!

In this chapter, I will attempt to break down how to get your classroom space organized to promote and embrace independent reading as well as reflect who you are as a teacher (because that is important, too). When I plan how I want to organize my classroom space, I consider the what, the when, and the how. By the *what*, I mean what actually needs to get organized—you know, all that stuff in your classroom. So, in the first section, I will discuss the organization of the classroom library as a focal point of your instructional space and then tackle how to organize the remainder of your space to promote independence and personal Zen. Next, the *when* will be addressed, and I will discuss how to organize your instructional time so these beautiful classroom spaces get used and refreshed routinely and purposefully. After all, who cares how fabulous your library is if no one *ever* gets to spend any time there? Finally, I will explore the *how*, describing how to organize the classroom routines in a way that will promote student independence within that space.

Organizing the Classroom Library

When asked, many of us would say that one of our primary goals as teachers of reading is to instill a love of reading in our students. But how can we do that if our classroom libraries are haphazardly organized or void of texts that excite and intrigue our students? The classroom library should be a focal point in any elementary school classroom. And it should be organized in such a way that it promotes excitement about books and independent student use. After all, sharing is caring, right?

If you have read a lot of the same books that I have about organizing your classroom library, your mind is probably filled with visions of kitschy table lamps, squashy pillows, and secondhand couches made fabulous again with just a little love and elbow grease. You may already feel inadequate as a teacher of reading because your room isn't big enough to accommodate furniture beyond student desks, you don't really get the whole table lamp thing, or you aren't pumped at the idea of scouring yard sales for used furniture to clean and restore. If any of this rings true, I ask you, what does any of this have to do with learning how to read and fostering a love of reading? In the wise words of Donalyn Miller (2009), one of my teaching idols, "I have never seen a student who became a reader because of access to a beanbag chair" (p. 66). If you are willing and able to create a cozy nook for reading that is worthy of the pages of *Better Homes and Gardens*, go for it. But if that cozy reading nook is not in your future for whatever reason, don't despair. Creating an environment that allows, supports, and encourages the growth of your students as readers is more about organization and text selection than it is about fabric swatches and the optimal bulb wattage.

I understand that organizing your classroom library space is a beast of a project. It is more challenging, time-consuming, and logistically difficult than anyone outside of a classroom can possibly imagine. However, it can and should be an integral piece of your instructional spaces, one that has the potential not only to promote excitement and independence in relation to reading but also to reflect the interests and tastes of both you and your students. To be honest with you, I have a love/hate relationship with my classroom library. I love the neat, organized, and colorful labels. I hate that lurking pile of books that I can never figure out where to shelve. I love the bursting baskets, filled with books, books, glorious books! I hate when books are put back in the wrong place, carelessly and without thought. I love watching my students use the library with confidence and independence. I hate vacuuming and maintaining the space (like the time I walked into my classroom to find a giant mouse carcass in the middle of my library rug). There were years when I felt as if I did not have enough books, and I spent more free moments than I can count hoarding Scholastic bonus points from student book orders, scouring yard sales, and looking for online deals or donations. Then, there were years that my principal ordered more books than I knew what to do with, and I sat hopelessly in a mountain of books, desperately trying to sort and organize. I often felt like I had created a situation in which I could never win: I either had too many books or not enough.

Let me paint you a picture of what a real teacher (a.k.a. me) looks like when organizing her classroom library space from a bunch of boxes to a bunch of fabulous: A teacher sits in a prominent corner of her classroom surrounded by boxes, empty bookshelves, a variety of buckets, a box of markers, packets of colored dots, index cards, tape, and several discarded iced coffees. Her hair is disheveled. Her fingers are cracked and riddled with paper cuts from opening box after box after box of books. (Be careful what you wish for when you wish for "more books.") She is covered with a sheen of sweat and wears a look of panic. Her colleague pops in.

Teacher: [with a crazed look in her eyes] I've spent the last two days trying to level and organize all my books.

Colleague: I know, it's brutal, right?

Teacher: I think I'm done, but now I need to organize all these other books into logical categories. Should I have an "oceans" basket, or is that weird? Should I just do animals, or do I need to break that down even more? Maybe I should just save those books for later? And what do I do with this one book about frogs? I have no other books about amphibians, but it can't go in a basket with snakes, right? Or do I rename the basket? [sips from iced coffee number 4 for the day]

Colleague: I think that maybe you need to step away from the books.

Sound familiar? The reality is that organizing your classroom library to be a pillar of perfection is a beast. It is hard, time-consuming, and often back-breaking work that takes more than just a few afternoons. Here are some of my tried-and-true, research-backed suggestions for creating an organized and joyful classroom library. I crafted this list with your sanity in mind, striving to create a process that doesn't drive you over the edge. (Fingers crossed!) If this still seems like too much to tackle in one sitting, map out an organizational plan with goals for today, next month, and perhaps six months from now. Then, promptly go and celebrate taking the first small step toward more organizational Zen.

Simmer Down Now: Tackle the Process in Phases

I know you want your library to be fabulous and picture-perfect tomorrow. In reality, it is a worthwhile project but a beast to complete. The key to getting started with the organization process is to set some realistic goals for organizing your library in phases. First, focus on leveling and labeling books for student independent reading selections. Accomplish that. Feel good. Then, move on to thinking about pulling out texts that reflect teaching from other areas of your day, such as math, science, and social studies. Create baskets and labels for those books. Accomplish that. Feel good. Now, move on to putting together logical special collections of books by looking for patterns in the books that are left. Do you have a lot of books by a particular author, in a particular series, or around a particular theme or topic? Organize these collections into labeled baskets. Accomplish that. Feel good. Then, if you are anything like me, you will still have a random assortment of books that don't really belong anywhere. Cut yourself some slack and put those books in a basket in the back of your closet to deal with another day. Sometimes you just have to call it a day on a project as enormous as organizing your classroom library.

As you make your way through this process, remind yourself of this little statistic when you feel a little overwhelmed: In a study of more than 350 schools, it was found that simply placing organized library spaces with a range of high-quality texts in classrooms increased student reading time by 60% (Neuman, 1999). Sixty percent, y'all! So, although it may be daunting, remember that this is a project that is well worth your time and energy.

Sort Your Books Into Logical, Easy-to-Use Categories

One trend that I have recently seen in many classrooms (and a trend that I do not believe is the fault of the teacher, by the way) is sorting and organizing books *only* by level. Don't get me wrong, leveling is a wonderful tool to use in the teaching of reading; knowing how books progress in difficulty along a continuum and being able to match those books to typical skills that students need to be successful with those books is kind of, well, hot. However, whether they are color coded, numbered, or organized à la Fountas and Pinnell (1999), it is still a huge wall of leveled books. Nothing else is identifiable with the organization of that intimidating wall to assist students in the selection of a book—no genre, no topic, no author, no interest, nothing that you will ever encounter in the real world. Just levels, levels, and more levels. I often wonder what this looks like from the perspective of the little friends in that classroom. Do they imagine the books mocking them, as if the books at higher levels are taunting them with you-can-look-but-you-can't-touch-me glances? Do they push readers to work harder? (My guess is no.) Do they make readers feel bad about where they are and limit their choices? (My guess is yes.) Levels are fabulous. They are a great tool and have shaped my own teaching of reading. However, does organizing a library exclusively by levels promote independence, a love of reading, and the skills necessary to access relevant materials outside the classroom? Um, no, it doesn't.

I suggest leveling roughly 25–30% of your classroom library. Although students can and should have access to books at their independent reading levels, particularly in the lower elementary grades, this suggested formula does not result in a library dominated by book levels and the corresponding implicit message that reading level is what matters most to readers. Rely on free resources, such as Scholastic's online Book Wizard (www.scholastic .com/bookwizard), for determining the level of each book. Create a simple system for organizing and labeling your books by level. Many teachers like using colored dots to represent different levels of books. For example, books at one level get a red dot, books at the next level get an orange dot, the books at the next level receive a yellow dot…I think you get the point. Take care to put a label on each book that will reside in the leveled basket as well as a clear label on the outside of the basket itself. Be generous with your use of clear packing tape to ensure that these labels stay on for more than two weeks. Only display books at those levels that are appropriate for your students at any given time. Other leveled baskets should be stored for later use.

For the remainder of your library, consider sorting your resources by genre, theme, author, series, text type, and/or subject matter. Other interesting categories of books to include are your own personal favorites ("Mrs. Scoggin's Faves" was a very popular place to search for new reading material in my classroom), award winners, and book collections curated by your students themselves. Remember, the classroom library is a space you share with your students. Although you are primarily responsible for how it is organized and the resources included within it, you want to create places for students to put their own mark on the feel of the library. Now, I'm not getting all unrealistic on you; I am merely suggesting leaving space for a few baskets that are organized by students. Perhaps they become a space to collect class favorites, favorite books of students who were born in a particular month, or favorites selected by a favorite out-of-the-classroom teacher. (Hey, the art and physical education teachers read, too.)

Include a Broad Range of Materials That Reflect Your Students' Interests and Reading Lives

Supporting my students as future readers means providing them with the tools and examples of texts that are reflective of the real reading and writing that people do outside of school. What types of materials we read when we are in school and how we read them can be vastly different from what and how we choose to read in our personal lives. Although books will always reign supreme in my heart, they may not be the top choice of text type for my students. The bottom line is that, as mentioned in Chapter 2, I don't care if students are reading a take-out menu as long as they are reading and reading something they love. (Maybe a room full of little friends reading take-out menus is not exactly the ideal, but I think you get what I mean.)

What does this mean for your classroom library? It means it is essential to consider the ideas, cultures, and genders that are reflected in our library collections. Students benefit from culturally responsive teaching, a facet of which is exposure to literature that represents a wide variety of cultures, people, places, and values (Blakeney-Williams & Daly, 2013; Dietrich & Ralph, 1995; Dowd, 1992; Gay, 2002; Rasinski & Padak, 1990; Rodriguez, 2014). We want all of our students to be able to see themselves represented in our libraries. We also want our students to get a wide view of the world and, therefore, use our text selections as windows beyond the classroom's specific community or the students' current experience.

In addition, including more contemporary material, such as graphic novels, traditional literature, and informational text, is also important. When woven into the classroom experience thoughtfully, increased access to informational text can help empower students to be active inquirers able to investigate topics independently (Maloch & Horsey, 2013). Regular access to informational text is also a powerful motivator to engage students while encouraging them to actively learn about the world around them (Calo, 2011). Finally, as we review our classroom library offerings, we must consider what and how students are actually reading as well as what and how they will be expected to read in the future. Access to tablets, e-readers, and/or computers to engage with digital texts is now something to consider seriously. Students must be able to regularly practice navigating and interacting with age-appropriate blogs, websites, and other digital texts. I know that this may sound like idealistic pie-in-the-sky talk that feels far beyond your reach and, if we are going to be blunt, unnecessary academic chatter. If I hit your nail on the head, then take a moment to reflect on your own reading life: What did you read today? I read several e-mails, glanced over my local newspaper, checked a train schedule, read a stack of picture books, scanned a new recipe, went digging through several academic articles, spent some time with my favorite blogs, scrolled through my Twitter feed, flipped through *People* magazine, and then turned (finally!) to my current pleasure reading. That is a lot of reading, and I'm sure I am leaving out quite a bit. If that is my reading reality, then I have a responsibility to question my own practices as a teacher of reading and wonder how I am preparing my students for this range of reading types and purposes in their own lives.

Although securing all of these types of texts and reading experiences may not be possible in each and every classroom (and because I do not advocate that you go out and spend every last dollar that you have earned on buying these items yourself), classroom libraries must work alongside school libraries to create a wide range of reading opportunities for children. Work with your school librarian to create more flexible lending policies or to find time when students can regularly visit this alternative, rich resource. Richard Allington and Patricia Cunningham (2007) write of the importance of wide access to both the classroom library and the larger school library, especially for students living in low–socioeconomic status neighborhoods who are less likely to live in print-rich environments or have access to an outside library facility.

Another tactic is to advocate for becoming more actively involved in your school's process for ordering new materials. Although I love to complain as much as the next teacher, we can only complain for so long. If you are unhappy with the books being ordered (or not ordered) for your classroom, get involved and make concrete suggestions for those titles and/or text types that would support your instruction and help refine this crucial space within your classroom.

Store Books and Other Print Resources in Clearly Labeled Baskets, Bins, or Buckets

Now that you've decided which books to include in your classroom library and how you want to organize and categorize them, it's time to get your container on. Place all of those lovely books into baskets, buckets, or bins and then add a clear and easy-to-read label to the front of each one.

I recommend that you use the same paper (I love unlined index cards), similar handwriting, and coordinated colors to maximize the look of your organization. Appearances matter. Consider placing a number on each basket and then using a small sticker to label each book within that basket with the same number so students can easily return a book to its proper place (meaning, not on the floor, behind a bin, or jammed into any old basket).

Organizing your classroom library in such a clear-cut manner enables students to independently utilize and maintain that space. It's a win–win scenario for everyone. Your students are easily able to access the library, to make their own choices as readers, and to use these materials when and how they see fit. At the same time, you no longer need to play police officer, housekeeper, or ringmaster and waste precious instructional time overseeing the use of your library. (I mean, if we wanted to be traffic cops, we would have become traffic cops instead of teachers, right?)

Be Proactive About Predictable Problems That Threaten Your Space

You know what I mean when I say, "predictable problems." The scene: Your classroom. A group of students is working in the library, selecting books for their independent reading. You are working with a small group. Everything is fabulous until one student encounters a book with ripped pages, marker on the front, or (gasp) a missing cover. Crisis! Under the guise of being helpful, said student rushes to your small group, disrupting any instructional magic you had going, and loudly announces that this particular book is in need of some serious first aid. "What do I do, Mrs. Scoggin? What do I do with this book?" cries the student "helper." Sound familiar?

Interruptions such as these are like kryptonite to your teacher happiness as well as the flow of your instruction. Although we can deal with several of these interruptions with patience, a smile, and gentle guidance, eventually these sorts of issues can make us want to claw our eyes out and be, shall we say, less than cheerful. Be proactive by creating spaces in your library for exactly these sorts of issues that creep up again and again, year after year, in classroom upon classroom. Create a "First Aid" basket for books that need some attention (read: tape and/or a good stapler). Create a basket for books that do not have an obvious home (read: The sticker fell off, and/or the student has blanked as to where it should go and is moments away from shoving it just anywhere). Create a basket for books that students want to talk to you about. Include a pencil and some sticky notes in this basket so your "helpers" can jot their comments to you without interruption. As other problems arise throughout the year, take a deep breath, grab an empty bucket, and proclaim, "There's a bucket for that!"

Create Inviting Book Displays

Let's be real with ourselves: When we walk into a bookstore, we spend time looking at and thinking about the books laid out in interesting displays on tables. Personally, I can admit to standing there thinking things such as, Ooh, these are so shiny, I should read these classics, or I guess it's time to stock up on some summer beach reading. If looking at well-curated collections of books motivates us to try something new or to think about books that we would like to place on our must-read lists, then why not try this approach with our students, too? Create inviting displays that draw attention to your most recent read-alouds, collections of books related to the season, an exciting new genre, your current unit of study in science or social studies, or an intriguing author or illustrator. By swapping out and refreshing these displays throughout the year, your library becomes an evolving and critical space within your classroom, growing and changing with the needs and interests of your students. Plus, looking at a new collection of shiny book covers in neat rows always made me smile as I glanced over at my library, and that is worth something in and of itself.

Refresh Your Space

Stagnant classroom library spaces are like bad wallpaper. They become a forgettable backdrop against which your day occurs rather than a vital part of your classroom. Let's face it: We all get bored with the same old same old after a while. Therefore, it's quite refreshing to you and your students when you can reserve some collections of books to rotate into your library over the course of the school year. Now, I know that this is easier said than done because one has to not only set these books aside but also *remember* to do this, which, in the midst of report cards, field trips, lesson planning, and data collecting, can easily slip your mind. My advice? While you are thinking about it (yes, right now), jot yourself a note to switch up the library. Now, put that note in your planner. Make another one and stick it in your planner or on your calendar two months from now. Rinse and repeat, and consider yourself reminded.

Many kids are able to sniff out a change in the classroom seconds after walking in. "Did you move that poster a bit to the left?" they ask as you stare at them incredulously. Other kids seem to move through the day in a fog and may not even notice if you painted the walls flaming red. It takes all kinds, right? Regardless, if you are going to put the time and effort into refreshing your classroom library space by placing out a new basket of books or creating a new display, honor that effort by spending a few minutes introducing the change to your students. Consider hosting a short book introduction or book sale in which you formally show off your hard work to your students. Spend five minutes showing off five of the new books included in this new collection—one minute for each book. Share the title, the author, a brief synopsis, and an idea of who might like to read this book or what other books it is similar to. The format that this introduction takes is up to you. Just keep it short and remember that the goal is to get students excited about new additions and to push them to select and try a wide range of books for themselves.

Another added bonus of reserving books to share later that alleviates a common problem in many classrooms is the classic syndrome of "I don't have enough space for all of these materials." (Between you and me, sometimes that mountain of books can be too intimidating to organize all at once. Don't beat yourself up about reserving a box to deal with at a later time. Just think of it as creating a surplus that you can dip into to keep your library choices fresh and interesting.) Classrooms fill up fast, and libraries have the potential to completely take over your room if you let them. So, keep some books stored away in the deep recesses of your closet. Pull them out when you come upon that lovely reminder note, and introduce them to your class. Get excited. Be nerdy. Take the opportunity to renew student excitement around this space that you have worked so hard to organize. Be proud of yourself for accomplishing this goal.

Organizing the Rest: Creating a Classroom Space That Celebrates You and Your Students

Just like your classroom library space, the remaining space in your classroom deserves careful consideration and purposeful planning, too.

The goal is to create a space that celebrates who you are as a teacher, who your students are, and what they have accomplished at any given point within the school year. Are you rolling your eyes and thinking, Is she *seriously* talking about a classroom space that is celebratory? I totally am. When I talk about a space that celebrates who you are as a teacher, I mean creating a classroom environment that reflects your personality, style, and interests. This can take the shape of simple items such as a basket of your favorite read-alouds, a corner with some of your personal items, or a rainbow theme on your bulletin boards. It can also take the shape of things that simply make you smile: a favorite pen or coffee mug, a stash of personal items or pick-me-up snacks, or a playlist stored on your computer with pump-you-up-after-school music for when your students are gone and you are faced with some major cleanup time. Although we are an important piece of the classroom community, the majority of our space should be reserved for celebrating our students. For me, this meant that my classroom walls were typically empty at the start of the year. Rather than fill my walls with posters and premade cutouts, I prepared and labeled spaces for future student work, making it clear to students that their efforts were the centerpiece of our community. I also intentionally left several spaces unfinished and turned to my new friends to help me make key decisions.

Maybe you love the way you set up your classroom space each and every year, or perhaps you set up your classroom a particular way because "I've always set it up this way." Either way, it is never a bad idea to prioritize, edit, and refresh your space. Although building routines that are supported by your classroom layout are key to smooth sailing during the school year, leaving everything exactly as it was on the first day of school can also mean that certain places and spaces become overlooked. Take note of spaces, charts, or resources that are underused by students and ask yourself the tough questions: Is this space meaningful to my students? Is it no longer a priority? Does it need to go or get refreshed?

Create Dedicated Spaces for Students to Share Their Work and Their Thinking

Not every bulletin board in your classroom has to be a major work of art that includes custom-cut bubble letters, a jaunty cartoon figure, and matching borders. Although it is important to create displays outside of classrooms that celebrate students' most polished efforts, inside the classroom, where displays are created for the benefit of you and your students and not outsiders, we want to create space with the primary purpose of displaying what students are doing and thinking *in the moment*. Our classrooms are places where we should celebrate the messiness of hard work and great thinking. It should be organized and attractive, of course, but the focus should be on what is timely and relevant to the classroom and not on something that looks pretty. In other words, say goodbye to the old, yellowing writing response that was composed two months ago but looks nice, so was kept up simply for that reason. Forget about asking students to mind-numbingly copy over their work in their best handwriting for the sole purpose of making the display look pretty; hang up and applaud the often messy look of a draft that has been lovingly revised and edited over time.

What exactly is it that I am suggesting? There are actually quite a few directions that this space could go. You could create a space where students can quickly post and share their thoughts about a text that they are currently reading. Or, you could create a space in which students are able to write and share their goals or struggles as readers, acknowledging the fact that everyone has struggles and goals. Another idea is to post a weekly question about your students' reading and a place for them to quickly respond. For example, you might ask, "Who is your favorite author? Why?" and provide students with sticky notes and markers to add their thoughts. Or, you might pose these questions: "What central idea or theme is addressed in the book that you are reading right now? What message do you think the author would like you to take away from the text?" Once students have posted several responses, take a few moments to work together to sort these responses by central idea or theme with the goal of promoting a new way for students to think about their reading selections or books to place on their must-read lists.

Use Your Walls Wisely
Classroom wall space is often in short order and in high demand. Whether your administration has strong opinions about what merits wall space or you are faced with more charts and posters than you can shake a stick at, only those artifacts that are routinely used by students should be

given priority. So, take a look around your classroom with a critical eye and prioritize. What resources, charts, posters, and diagrams can you confidently confirm as useful to your students as they work independently? Before you can change your mind, remove everything that is simply taking up space and not serving a purpose. I mean it. Introduce feng shui on your walls. Believe me, I know how hard this is. We are teachers (read: probable pack rats), and for many of us, throwing things away is hard.

Now, did you just take down some artifacts that have a lot of potential but were simply forgotten about? Before you throw the baby out with the bathwater, consider editing these resources. Do you need to spice them up with a few visuals, photographs, or student examples? Can you involve students more meaningfully in creating some of these same artifacts in the future? Do you need to model relying on these resources more often in your instruction? After all, we know that most students will not just spontaneously turn to a word wall unless that sort of effort is repeatedly modeled for them time after time. Take a moment and consider editing these resources before reintroducing them to your class as useful tools.

Just like the student work on your walls, any artifacts of your instruction should also reflect current endeavors. Keep in mind that even though a process chart was once an instructional masterpiece, it may be time for that particular product of your genius to retire. Alternatively, you may want to store these resources in a clearly marked space so if students really do want to remind themselves of, say, how to determine the key points of a piece of informational text, they can do so independently and with confidence. It's up to you. Either way, when someone walks into your classroom, it should be fairly obvious what you are working on as readers right now (not last month).

Don't Be Afraid to Get Personal

I know it seems like everyone and their brother is trying to standardize our work. What they don't seem to realize is that the act of teaching is deeply personal and involves making strong connections with our students. I truly don't think it's possible to create these types of relationships or a caring classroom environment without sharing pieces of who you are as a person and a learner.

Although classroom spaces should mostly be about and for the students in your classroom, there is certainly room and reason for including a bit of yourself and your own personality. I like to have a book I am currently reading out for students to see, a small photo wall of people and places that are important to me, and a basket of grade-level–appropriate books by authors I love or about topics I care deeply about. For example, we always found time in my classroom to study the works of specific illustrators and to create art pieces inspired by those illustrators because I love art and I love the illustrations in children's literature. Did I have to ground a lot of my instruction in the standards to justify the time I allocated to this work? Of course I did. Regardless of anyone's opinion, education today is permeated by methods of accountability, standards, and rigor. But instead of letting those realities overwhelm and stifle our creativity and moments of personal Zen, shouldn't we spend time finding ways to view the types of projects and instruction we believe in with whatever new lens is currently being touted?

When modeling strategies for reading informational text, I almost always read about elephants because I love elephants. When composing a model piece of persuasive writing I almost always thought and wrote about animal advocacy issues because I have a special place in my heart for animals living in shelters. My students know these things about me, and they should. If I expect them to share all of their thoughts, struggles, frustrations, and hard work with me, I should do the same. I am not and will never be just a body at the front of the room.

Organizing the Instructional Time You Spend in Your Space

Having a beautiful and well-organized classroom space is fabulous. However, one key piece to having a well-organized classroom space that actually functions is thinking about the times when students engage with these various places and spaces within your room. You guessed it: It's time to talk about how to organize your instructional time so students get an opportunity to explore that gorgeous library you sweat over.

Every time I sat down in front of my planner to organize my week, the issue of insufficient time in the day made me feel frustrated. I recall one week in particular when I felt particularly overwhelmed after trying my hardest to fit it all in. And by "fit it all in," I mean include each of the demands placed on me by the administration with regards to every subject area I taught. Let's see, 20 minutes for a morning meeting; 60 minutes for math; 90 minutes for reading instruction; a 45-minute block each for content area instruction, lunch, and gym; 60 minutes of writing; 25 minutes of word study; 10 minutes for dismissal procedures; and, oh, 30 minutes for that guy to come in and provide my class with recorder lessons. (I know. *I know.*) When I added it all up, that came to a grand total of 430 minutes, or exactly 40 more minutes than I had in the actual school day. These are indeed the things that make you go, "Hmmm." However, this week in particular, I did not simply go, "Hmmm." Instead, I marched to my assistant principal's office, explained to her the situation, and asked very matter-of-factly, "What would you do?" Her words of wisdom? "I know you'll make it work." To which I promptly turned on my heel and added 40 minutes to the instructional day, changed around the bus schedule, and gained permission from all the parents of the students in my class. No, wait. That's not what I did. I left her office, put my head down on my desk in my classroom, and cried a little. Dealing with time constraints certainly did not make me happy, that's for sure.

I know I am not alone in this. The pressure of time constraints is continually cited as a source of major teacher stress (Brown & Ralph, 1998; Carlyle & Woods, 2002; Klassen & Chiu, 2010; Kyriacou, 1998; Rousmaniere, 1997; Walsh, 1998). In one study, it was found that when under stress, teachers often make decisions based on the priorities of their administration rather than on their own instructional priorities or expertise (Lasky, 2005). So, let's take a moment, take a deep breath, and think about the priorities for instructional time that reflect best practices in reading instruction. Although we may not be able to implement these guidelines exactly as they are written, we can still use them to guide our decisions about time and as support for our conversations with administrators when and if we are asked to explain our choices. Remember, there is no point in organizing the space if you don't also organize the time children will spend in those spaces.

So, let's start thinking (or rethinking) about how you use your time for reading instruction, shall we? There are a few major ways we can think about this to promote student independence (and your own Zen—can't forget about that!) in your classroom.

Time to Read, Just Read

It may sound like a no-brainer, but you would be surprised at how little instructional time is devoted to letting students read. I am not sure how we expect students to become better readers if we don't provide them with time to, you know, read. I certainly did not get to be a better cook simply by listening to someone talk about cooking. (To my husband, no comments from the peanut gallery about my cooking, please.) I also did not get to be a better photographer by hearing someone talk about taking pictures. I got better at those things by practicing them. I made mistakes, and then I improved my abilities with guidance and support from others.

Allington (2012) doth proclaim that 90 minutes a day is the ideal amount of time for children to be reading in classrooms. Now, I know that you may not have 90 minutes to devote solely to independent reading in your classroom, and I get that. A girl can dream, though, can't she? So, if you don't have 90 minutes, what do you do? I suggest immediately devoting *at least* half of your reading instructional time to independent reading. Yes, this might mean that you may have to cut back on your whole-class direct reading instruction. However, may I remind you of my aforementioned cooking and photography examples? I am sure you are brilliant and quite entertaining, but no one can become a better reader simply by listening to you talk about it. They need a chance to practice what you're preaching.

A key component to this independent reading time is allowing students to self-select books from your now uber-organized classroom library. (See, it all comes full circle!) Although we naturally want to guide students toward books that they will most likely be successful with, basing these decisions on reliable data such as a running record, we want to allow students to choose their own books within their independent reading levels. The aspect of choice is a strong motivator to get student reading. According to Allington (2013), "the actual volume of reading activity is an important component in the development of a myriad of reading proficiencies" (p. 526). More plainly said, the more kids read, the more proficient they will become. Readers get to be stronger readers by reading (Allington, 2013; Hiebert, 2009). Putting in a little sweat to upgrade or reorganize your classroom library is totally worth it when you think of those rewards.

Even if you are able to build in a significant amount of time for students to read their own self-selected texts, you are probably going to struggle to hit the magical 90-minute mark. Therefore, try to find other ways to tack on additional time for students to read independently. Maybe they can pull out a book and read as soon as they walk in the door until everyone is ready for the day to begin. Encourage students to carry a book with them at all times so they can read while waiting in line with their parents at the grocery store; during car, subway, or bus rides (if they can stay vomit free and do this); or otherwise find themselves with a few spare moments. Are there other moments of instructional fat in your day? How about those 20 minutes you plan on using for settling down your class after they come back from recess? Direct students to pull out a book and read until you are ready to begin your afternoon. Or, try this: Sit down and read a book yourself as the class settles down and then see what happens. (You may be surprised at the interest students have in your personal reading life as well as how catchy your love of reading can be when it is authentic and put on display in purposeful ways.) And what about the seemingly endless parade of classroom interruptions that come in the form of announcements, pop-in visitors, or some nonteacher coming to your door with an unimportant and last-minute request? Make it a class rule that students pull out a book and read during these times.

One of my favorite class challenges was to tally just how many minutes we were able to read independently each day. Not only did it motivate students to stay focused and read longer, but it also sent them a clear message that I valued how long they spent with their eyes in a book. I was surprised by the creative moments children found to squeeze in more reading when increasing our volume of reading was made a priority. More effective teachers find more time for their students to read. So, as those minutes pile up, bask in the joy that is knowing you're doing the right thing for your students.

Meet Students' Individualized Instructional Needs During Independent Reading

Still not convinced that reading for the sake of reading is a good enough use of your instructional time? What if I told you that incorporating more independent reading time will also enable you to find time to focus on how to better meet your students' individualized instructional needs? If I may speak for all of us, rock star teachers like you and I feel our most Zen, effective, and, well, awesome when we are accomplishing goals, connecting with students, and pushing student growth. So, while your kiddos are reading, make your way around your beautifully organized classroom space and hold one-on-one instructional conferences or meet with small groups. Occasionally, look up and bask in the beauty that is a class full of readers working in a space that allows them to be independent, and allow yourself a moment to smile.

To facilitate your ability to move around the classroom efficiently, let's take a moment and talk about—you guessed it—the physical space you created! Group student desks or work tables together in small clusters with ample space for you to move about between them. If you are meeting with students one on one as they read independently, go to them, dragging a chair along behind you. Going to them, rather than calling them to a remote corner, allows you to spread your influence around the classroom. Not only will your presence at a given table encourage better behavior while reading, but other students also may listen in (and learn something) as you discuss various reading goals and strategies with a student.

As far as meeting with small groups of students during this independent reading time, this is a moment for using an alternative space. Set up a small table or a cluster of desks with chairs to meet with small groups. You only need six chairs (and one for yourself) because more than six students does not a small group make. Take care to create a small teacher space within this small-group setting so you can have your materials for the group ready ahead of time. Nothing disrupts your Zen (and wastes instructional time) more than looking for the book that you intended to share or that piece of paper—or I swear I had a marker over here! I love a simple pencil box for storing essentials such as pencils for student use, markers, pens, sticky notes, and index cards. That, combined with a small tray for keeping any essential papers or books organized, works wonders.

Sharing Is Caring

Time and again, teachers tell me that reading books aloud to their students is one of their greatest pleasures. I couldn't agree more, and I totally do a mean read-aloud. We are talking about a full-blown dramatic performance. Sharing a beloved book with my little friends always brought joy to my crushed teacher soul on those difficult days when it felt like there was no end in sight to the interruptions and pointless meetings.

Regardless of your personal level of dramatic finesse, we are teachers of reading. We love books—and reading. Yet, in many classrooms I have been in, read-alouds are often seen as a bonus or add-on to regular literacy instruction—you know, something fun that you get to when you have time. However, when planned purposefully, read-alouds can fit into almost any area of the day and be a powerful instructional tool. Reading aloud to our students (including you, upper elementary friends) is an essential part of classroom practice. According to one of my favorite teachers of reading, Debbie Miller (2002), reading aloud is key to motivating students to want to learn to read. It is during a ritualistic read-aloud that we are able to model fluent reading; make our thinking public for students; and expose students to a wide variety of complex texts, text types, and genres. Well-chosen read-alouds can enhance student vocabulary, build background knowledge, and encourage students to think critically. It is also during these sacred times that we are able to establish a sense of community and an intimate sharing of a love for books and reading. When we share the books we love most with our students, we model a love and enthusiasm for reading. Share the joy, my friends, share the joy.

I spend a lot of time with a lot of teachers. I'm lucky that way. Almost every teacher I talk to proclaims a love of reading aloud to his or her students. However, these same teachers also admit that when they are strapped for time (and who isn't?), their read-aloud is the first thing to go. I get it. It may often seem that there are never enough hours in the day for read-alouds (even though there are also days when the end can't seem to come fast enough). Our decisions about how to use our time and space should be guided by what we know to be best instructional practices. I know that many of you out there feel as if your hands are tied and that your schedules are determined for you (and without you). Yet, we can no longer in good conscience stand idly by, shut our doors, and complain to our colleagues. Building a community of readers through read-alouds is an essential component in creating a strong literacy block (Miller, 2014), and therefore, we should preserve and advocate for this time in our daily schedules.

Putting It All Together: Establishing Clear Routines

Tell me the truth: The second I started yammering on about organizing your classroom library into labeled baskets, some of you immediately thought, That's all good and well, but in two weeks, it will be a disaster again. Come on, I can take it. So, instead of throwing in the towel, let's consider what routines you can implement to allow students freedom and choice in the library while decreasing the likelihood of a free-for-all.

Everybody loves a good routine, right? Routines bring order, stability, and predictability and help to alleviate potential behavioral problems. In general, I believe that strong, well-established, and purposeful routines help your classroom hum with productivity, allowing you to focus on the work of teaching new material and students to use the classroom space effectively. Student ownership, combined with regular use and strong routines, equals respect and responsibility when it comes to helping maintain the classroom library. Creating routines that expect your students to participate meaningfully in the upkeep of your classroom library is key, as well as allowing students to have a voice in future additions or new routines.

The start of the school year is the ideal time to think about, create, teach, and practice clear routines that will set you up for the rest of the school year. Now, if you are reading this in the middle of the year and having a mild panic attack that your organizational ship has sailed, don't fret! If your current systems feel as if they are not as effective as you'd like them to be or you are struggling to bring organization to a particular piece of your day, anytime is the right time. Remember, we are problem *solvers* (not just problem posers), and we can solve an organizational problem at any time of the year. If only the title of "problem solver" came with a cape, we would be true superheroes! Anyhow, regardless of the time of year, the routines you could potentially integrate into your practice are endless (insert quiver of nerdy joy here), but for the sake of brevity, let's just discuss three routines that promote using and maintaining your classroom space.

Routines for Lending Books to Students

We know that more lenient library lending policies are important (Allington, 2013), particularly for students who have less regular at-home access to text. We also know that many parents, despite the best of intentions, struggle to select appropriate material for their children. Matching texts to readers is hard, which is why sending students home with material to read from our beautifully organized classroom libraries is essential. Take a deep breath and accept right now that some books will get lost. Some books will get damaged. I know that there are few things sadder than a mistreated book, but I believe that a book that has never been read is sadder still.

Consider having your students practice bringing home something less valuable than your precious (and expensive!) books before sending home the real deal. For example, if you are ultimately going to send books back and forth in a ziplock bag, have students practice carrying a letter outlining your library policies each night for a week. Every night, parents must read and discuss your library policies with their child, signing the letter to be returned to school the next day. Although this won't solve all of your lending issues, at least you have led the proverbial horse to the water. You might also consider having students carry small, easily reproducible books (e.g., those found on Reading A–Z at www.readinga-z.com) back and forth to practice your routines and build more responsible habits. Regardless, think about what you would like students to carry their books in and where you would like students to place their books once they return to school each morning. Establish, discuss, and practice these routines with reckless abandon until you are confident in your students' level of comfort.

Routines for Spending Time in the Library

For lower grade students, aim to provide small groups of children with a routine time to interact with your classroom library at least two times a week. During one of these visits, students should be tasked with swapping out their independent text selections for new texts. Take care to spend time with children during the early weeks of practicing this routine. Your presence is necessary to help students understand how your library is organized and to coach into their ability to self-select appropriate titles. Be clear about the choices available to students and the number of books you would like them to borrow on a weekly basis. As a rule of thumb, students should have enough independent reading material to sustain them across a week, allowing for some rereading of text. During the other visit, students should be free to engage with the remaining portion of your library in whatever way they choose. This might mean partner reading Big Books, digging into an informational text about horses, or scrolling through a kid-friendly website, such as National Geographic Kids (kids.nationalgeographic.com).

For upper elementary students, allow more flexibility and ownership of this routine. Perhaps students are free to visit the classroom library as they see fit to exchange their independent reading selections but are required to do so at least once within a certain period of time. Set a rule that no more than five or six students are allowed in the classroom library in order to minimize noise and distraction. Regardless, routines should be clear, predictable, and practiced regularly to ensure maximum independence. Although you want to be perceived as a lover of books, you never want to become the ultimate keeper (and hoarder) of the books.

Routines for Keeping the Library Organized

Make it a classroom job or responsibility for one or more students to spot-check and resolve any issues within several baskets on a weekly basis. Place a small card in the back of each basket so students can initial and date when the basket is checked to ensure that a variety of baskets are looked at over time. Also consider adding a wish list in your library so students can request or suggest titles for future purchases. This wish list can be distributed to families for possible donations and to the parent–teacher organization within your school and used to help direct future purchasing of materials as your school budget allows.

Despite your best-laid plans, your classroom library is bound to need a little touch-up from time to time. You just don't want to spend a ton of time every single week straightening and restraightening because, you know, there are a zillion other things that need your attention. However, letting your library fall into total disrepair sends the unintended message that it is not a vital or important space within your classroom. So, what do you do? Set a time once a month—every last Tuesday or every third Wednesday, for example—to evaluate the selections in your library, refresh the options or displays included, and spot-check several baskets on your own. Make it a rule. Sit down and write a reminder on a sticky note. Now, count forward in your planner and add this little gem so you don't forget. Stick to it. Then, promptly reward yourself with a new pen, a tasty dessert, a yummy cocktail, or (my personal favorite) some fancy shoes. Even I can admit that sometimes simply checking an item off a to-do list isn't enough.

Organization Is a Beautiful Thing

I want to end my tirade on organization with a little story: I once had a student that we shall call Curly. Curly was a mischievous but incredibly bright little boy who had (and still has) a very special place in my teacher heart. Even though he was a good reader, Curly was a bit of a reluctant reader. Slowly but surely, we figured out what sorts of books he liked and the authors he enjoyed best. At the end of the school year, he begged me to let him take home some books to read over the summer. What was I supposed to say? "No, those books belong to me"? Of course, I said yes, and he hit the library with confidence and a bit of reckless abandon (I told you, he was on the naughty side). On the third day of school that following school year, he showed up at the door of my classroom with a rumpled ziplock bag filled with those same books. He looked at me with wide eyes and said, "Thank you for these. They made my summer." And then, without letting me say a single word, he marched over to my classroom library and reshelved his books. "You are all about organization, aren't you, Mrs. Scoggin?"

Yes, sweetheart, I am. Thanks for noticing.

CHAPTER 4

Let's Get Analytical

How to Approach and Survive Reading Assessment

> *Don't let them defeat you. Do what you have to do; in the end no one can mandate how you feel about children, the ways you interact with them throughout the day, and the things you say and do that reflect who you are and what you believe about teaching and learning.*
>
> —Debbie Miller (2008, p. 20)

Here is a little game for you: Go stand in a room full of teachers, shout out, "Assessment! Data! Standardized testing! Accountability!" and see what reactions you get. Few other words will evoke quite the same response, which can vary from eye rolling to full-on gagging sounds and, on a bad day, perhaps a thrown chair. But how did assessment go from being such a crucial educational tool to striking fear and exhaustion in the hearts of teachers everywhere? How has everything gotten so out of whack, and how can we possibly get teaching back on track?

As we made our way into the 21st century, accountability was a primary focus of reform ideas in the United States (Ravitch, 2010). Standardized testing began to control the curriculum and teaching by shifting the focus of schools to higher test scores rather than actual effective educational strategies, implying that test scores alone indicated success and were indicators of best practices. But you and I both know that this puts our priorities all out of order; the curriculum should lead the way for testing. Yet, somehow, we have found ourselves in this place where the curriculum is often following tests. Such trends, driven by a fidelity perspective that prioritizes the notion that all teachers should be on the same page at the same time, rob teachers of the ability to cater instruction to the needs of their students and to show evidence of their own beliefs in their practice, and simultaneously silence the voice of teachers as experts on their students' progress. Test scores now speak louder than words.

> When business and the world of commerce are permitted to invade the precincts of our public schools, not merely in the ancillary and familiar role of civic allies or occasional philanthropists but as participants in the determination of the aims of education and the content of instruction, they bring with them a body of beliefs and biases....
>
> Corporate leaders, when they speak of education, sometimes pay lip-service to the notion of "good critical and analytic skills," but it is reasonable to ask whether they have in mind the critical analysis of *their* priorities. (Kozol, 2005, p. 106)

Increasingly, school reformers have also turned to business models in an effort to find new directions for the improvement of public education.

Using business vocabulary and concepts, a variety of efficiency-driven, top-down policies and evidence-based models of instruction have been created and implemented in schools. These types of policies decrease the power and influence held by teachers. Ironically, teachers are charged with a massive responsibility to socialize and educate future generations yet are given little to no control over their own work (Ingersoll, 2007). Rather than using assessments to look across districts for informative patterns or as a tool to drive instruction, we are currently looking to assessments to rate the effectiveness of teachers while turning a blind eye to other confounding factors in students' success, such as poverty, equity in access to instructional resources, and level of parental involvement.

The sad reality is that the professional lives of teachers, and often teaching itself, are too frequently defined by everyone other than actual teachers. Beyond that, changes in major school policies are orchestrated by others outside of the classroom (Britzman, 1991; Goodwin, 1987). For some reason, educators have not retained a place at the policymaking table. Instead, we are placed in the position of enacting policy determined by a variety of individuals outside the classroom. And is it just me, or does it seem as if these policies change *every five minutes*? Friends, like it or not, we are a politically trendy target that is now subject to shifting in the political breeze. Educational policymaking has become such a popular political tool (Hess, 1999) that it has resulted in a wide range of experimentation in reform over time. More influenced by political pressures to create change than educational considerations, topical school reform efforts such as these have become so politically trendy that one particular policy may quickly be contradicted by or replaced with another. Hess refers to this phenomenon as policy churn. If you are anything like me, you can literally feel the churn from within the walls of your own classroom.

The current overemphasis on assessments, combined with the extreme high stakes placed on their outcomes, has created a perfect storm in which many teachers feel as if their hands are tied. Some teachers have sadly reported spending up to one quarter of their instructional year preparing for and administering assessments (Kozol, 2005). One quarter! As an example, I remember planning out the timing of the assessments I was required to administer in one month. My list included the following:

- A running record for each student
- A set of formal formative assessments for our current unit of study
- A sight word fluency test
- A nonsense word fluency test
- A decoding test
- A phonemic awareness assessment
- A comprehension assessment
- A benchmark spelling assessment

That's *eight* assessments in *one* month! Let's break this down, shall we? In a calm instructional month (meaning, one without snow days, assemblies, or field trips), there are roughly 20–22 instructional days. That is roughly one assessment every 2.75 days if each assessment only takes one day to administer, and that does not factor in time to correct or analyze the assessment. Say what? Beyond the issue of the amount of instructional time it takes to administer all of these assessments, there is little to no conversation about using this mountain of data to guide my instruction. Sure, I know it's best practice, and I will do my darndest to make some of these numbers and graphs relevant to my instructional plans so that this doesn't all feel like a colossal waste of time. But I wonder why the practical *use* of data beyond simply comparing one group of children with another is often left out of the conversation or, at best, mentioned in passing.

All of this assessment can and does feel exhausting, frustrating, and disheartening. So, what is a reading teacher to do? Continue to sweat through all of her shirts and scream in frustration behind the closed doors of a colleague? Probably. But after sufficiently venting, we can use all of that energy in a first step toward defining what it means to be a teacher focused on best practices by shifting our own thinking about the assessments continually piled on our plates. After too much time stewing in my own frustration, I want to share with you how I first began to reshape my thinking in the face of assessment overload and take back a sense of control of my own classroom in the hope that you will not waste as much energy on the frustration as I did. Then, I have some hard-earned suggestions on how you can refocus your own energy to reclaim teacher happiness and, in fact, breathe new life into your instruction despite the barrage of assessments that so often dominate our practice.

How I Reshaped My Own Approach to Assessments

Let's take a moment and just be honest about data collection and testing, shall we? In so many ways, it stinks. It's as simple as that. In my view, it dominates too much of our practice, too much of our time, and too many of our professional conversations. However, I want to share with you a story about testing that shaped my thinking about how to approach the barrage of mandated tests I confront on a regular basis.

Imagine my sweet little classroom. Normally, my little friends sit at desks arranged in collaborative groups, but one not-so-fine day, my friends had to sit in single rows. These were rows I had to waste precious instructional time teaching them how to form because of an insane administrative demand that thou shalt re-create the testing environment. I had just passed out a mandatory literacy assessment that asked my second-grade friends (whose reading levels span early first grade all the way through mid–third grade) to read 40 (yes, 40!) paragraphs about incredibly mundane and unfamiliar mindlessness and then answer multiple-choice questions. In true assessment style, students had to transfer their answers to a separate bubble sheet. As many of you who teach second grade may already know, this is akin to asking them to climb Mount Everest in flip-flops. Want to know the best part? Each child had to sit with the test until they all finished each and every question. For some students, this meant sitting there with a glaring beacon of their reading struggles in front of them for over an hour while those who finished (or *thought* they were finished) were made to sit in silence as their youth and love of reading slowly ticked away. I was not allowed to grade the assessment myself and would not receive the results of said assessment for several weeks, rendering its data pretty much useless in terms of directing my instruction.

Are you crying yet or at least sitting there mouth agape?

During this appalling ordeal, I walked over to a little friend who struggles in reading (and by "struggles," I mean substantially), noticing that he had his head down on his desk. "Are you OK?" I asked. My friend looked up with tears streaming down his face and replied, "I can't do anymore, Mrs. Scoggin. I just can't. I'm sorry." To which I said, "I know it's tough, sweetheart, but just do your best. That's all you can do, and you should never apologize for that." "But the words are just too hard. I'm not smart enough," he said. Holding back my own tears, I tried again: "Just try a few more, and then I promise you can stop. Don't worry about finishing." "And then can we go back to learning? I want to get to be a better reader," he said, looking at me with big brown eyes shining. "Yes, honey, then we'll go back to learning."

I mean, *come on!* It was in that moment that I decided to take a stand in the face of the testing that I felt went far above and beyond what was necessary and was, frankly, damaging to learning. I wish I could say that I staged some sort of political movement and was able to talk some sense into the powers that be, thereby changing the face of testing forever, but I can't. I began my resistance by marching into a colleague's room after school, shutting the door, and venting like no one has ever vented before. We are talking sweat-through-your-shirt-have-to-lie-down-when-you're-done venting. It felt cathartic. (You should try it if you haven't already. You deserve it.) But I knew that venting alone wasn't enough. I didn't want to get sucked into the shame spiral of complaining without taking action. To survive as a teacher and to even attempt to be happy while doing it (imagine that), I knew I had to change my attitude toward assessment and work to take back some sense of control, at least in my own classroom. So, that's what I did. And you can do it, too.

Focusing Your Energy on the Assessments That *Do* Help Shape Your Practice

The realities of assessment and data collection in today's classroom can quickly rob you of any and all inner Zen and leave very little time for those parts of the job that we truly love. None of us wants to teach to the test, none of us wants to be obsessed with the results of the most recent assessment, and none of us wants to allow the barrage of tests that we are required to administer to dominate our instructional time, yet somehow there are days and weeks during which assessment reigns supreme.

However, there *are* forms of data that are incredibly useful and help teachers better tailor their instruction to meet the needs of their students. Not one of the teachers I know (or at least none of the cape-worthy teachers I know) minds collecting data that feels purposeful. Sure, it is always a bit of an organizational challenge, but some of us who trend toward the type A personality don't mind an organizational challenge. The problem is that these worthwhile assessments become overshadowed by the seemingly endless list of mandated, less useful (dare I say, worthless) assessments. If you are unable to stay strong and true to your beliefs, it is very easy to find yourself simply distributing and collecting assessments without ever finding the time to analyze or utilize the data in meaningful ways. Basically, you become a human Scantron machine, and suddenly all of your free time is used to demonstrate your ability to enter data on a graph rather than to create dynamic lessons or, you know, *teach*.

So, how do you recapture the purpose and joy (yes, joy) of monitoring the progress of your students in smart ways? It would be lovely to simply boycott those assessments that you find to be pointless, but I am fairly certain that will not happen anytime soon, although you are welcome to take any and all political action on the side. Simply stewing in our own bitter juices won't do either. It all comes back to your thoughts about what it means to be a teacher and the type of classroom you would like to create for your students. (See? That old Education 101 Philosophy of Teaching statement comes in handy.) Take a critical look at the implementation and outcomes of each assessment you are required to give. Which assessments yield information that will help you refine your practice in important ways? Which ones result in data that are less helpful and most likely will end up just getting filed?

For me, this meant focusing on assessments that helped me truly better understand my students as readers so I could move our relationship forward. To do this, I needed data that allowed me to set reasonable short- and long-term goals for reading instruction and organize my class into appropriate small groups for more targeted work. Running records have always yielded this sort of data for me, so the organization, implementation, and analysis of these assessments won a great deal of my attention. Another key piece of my philosophy is holding my students accountable for my teaching in appropriate ways. Anecdotal records of my teaching were therefore key, and voila! I knew it was important for me to devote energy to record keeping during one-on-one student reading conferences and small-group work. Finally, reflecting critically on my own practice to improve my delivery of reading content from year to year and lesson to lesson is a huge component to the type of teacher I want to become. As a result, I prioritize both formal and informal formative assessments to help me monitor my students' level of understanding while immersed in a reading unit of study.

Once you have determined which assessments are most critical to your instruction, focus on those and allow the others to simply be items on your to-do list. Yes, you still have to do them, but, for me at least, it was easier to allocate those less worthwhile assessments to the space in my brain that I reserved for cleaning up mouse poo in my classroom. I don't love to do it, I never envisioned myself as a teacher doing it, but I do it anyway, and that's that.

Being Transparent With Students About Purpose: It's All in the Delivery

I believe in authentic teaching. That means not only creating authentic opportunities for students to share their learning and allowing them to choose authentic texts to read but also being authentic as a person. I am pretty much the same person in front of my students as I am with my friends—maybe minus some choice language and a cocktail. Students can see right through a fake persona. The way I see it is that you have to be real with them if you want them to let you in and be real with you.

So, let's be honest with our students about testing and its purpose. It's all in the delivery. Give an assessment (rather than hide it). Tell students you just want to see what they can do now so you better understand how to help them in the future. If you know it, show it. If you don't, don't sweat it. In many classrooms, there is too much anxiety around testing of any sort and a huge preoccupation with "being right." Students are afraid to get anything wrong or to perform poorly, and I wonder if trying to be Sneaky Sneakerson by camouflaging assessments may be partially to blame. Hiding assessments and not talking honestly about the purpose behind those meaningful assessments that help shape our work with children is a mistake. It should be one of our primary goals to create a culture in which students feel safe to take risks and are able to celebrate their successes while also acknowledging their struggles.

Too many times, I have seen students sit with a teacher to complete a formal running record with the sole purpose of "passing" or "getting to the next level." I then turn to see a classroom library dominated by clearly leveled texts, sending the message that we learn to read to get to a higher level rather than to learn or enjoy intriguing texts. Yes, we want our students to move on to more and more complicated and dynamic texts; however, we cannot present moving on to the next level as a motivator. The reason we give assessments to our students is to monitor their progress and to set clear goals for future teaching. We want our students to grow as readers so they might engage with text and the world in meaningful ways. What is wrong with sharing this stance with our students? Tell your students that it is important to let any assessment truly reflect their current understanding. Together, you can set goals for their reading and move them toward greater independence.

Students are learning by watching what we do as teachers as well as the elements we include in our classrooms. Create the opportunity for all students to build their ability to reflect on their own reading lives, while simultaneously reinforcing the idea that every reader has successes and struggles by posting these ideas publicly. Ask students to think carefully about their lives as readers: What feels good? What feels difficult? You may need to model an appropriate response to both of these questions. OK, you may need to *repeatedly* reflect this sort of thinking before you can expect students to knock this out of the park. However, after a bit of modeling and perhaps some shared writing experiences, students can begin to record their reflections in writing to be shared with the rest of the class.

One idea is to have students jot their successes and struggles as readers on an index card that gets taped to their desk. By making students' reflections public, we can kill two birds with one stone. Not only is this a way to acknowledge that everyone, no matter what type or level of reader, has successes and goals, but it also encourages students to rely on one another for advice. For example, some of my students became "famous" as experts in reading mysteries, so when another friend encountered a mystery that was confusing, he could turn to his mystery-loving friend (as opposed to shouting my name repeatedly until I stopped my reading conference). I say that's a win–win scenario.

Assessing Yourself to a Happier You: Using Meaningful Assessments to Feel Successful and Optimistic

How can assessing help you become a happier teacher? At first thought, this seems like a bananas idea, right? More often than not, when a teacher receives a compliment on anything—from his or her classroom, to the progress of students, to a recent lesson—the teacher is quick to shrug off the compliment, instead attributing the success to another factor. Here's a quick example: Your classroom library is thoughtfully organized, always full of fresh texts, and a central element to your practice. Your administrator notices and says, "Your library is a thing of beauty. I really appreciate how well organized it is. You are really promoting student independence and excitement about reading in that space." You say, "Oh, well, it's not me. The kids really help shape the library. It's really all them." Um, friend? Just say, "Thank you!" Sure, the kids probably do help you, but they wouldn't do that without your vision and guidance! Own your fabulousness, if not for yourself, then to model for your little friends that it is a wonderful thing to own your accomplishments.

So, how does assessment fit into all of this celebration of *you* and all things fabulous? It forces you to stop and take note of the learning that is happening around you. Often we are caught up in the day-to-day activities—lesson plans, homework packets, notes home, and read-alouds—and do not truly notice the amazing growth of our students. When you give an assessment, either formal or informal, you are forced to slow down and analyze the fruits of your labor. Take a minute and celebrate before you move on to thinking about anything else. Seriously, you are busy, but you aren't *that* busy. Who has moved to the next level as a reader? Who is reading with greater fluency? Who has discovered a new genre or author to love? Who is suddenly turned on by reading? You did that. OK, literally the kids did that, but you had a huge hand in their progress as readers. That is amazing!

Now, I know many of you are thinking, Yeah, that's nice to celebrate those students who made obvious progress, but what about our friends who are stalled, who don't love reading? I hear you. Of course, you are thinking about these little friends who struggle as readers. Assessing these students is not a time for despair and frustration. It is time to reframe your view to see assessment as an opportunity to refine your goals for those students and to create a new plan, reinvigorated by your recent observations, for future instruction. It is a time for optimism and a time for you to flex your teacher muscle by getting creative with your plan to address these needs. Research on workplace stress, particularly the research that deals with schools specifically, finds that teachers "who have greater opportunity for skill use are mentally more healthy than colleagues with little opportunity" (Walsh, 1998, p. 18). Use your skills! Show everyone what a rock star you are! We don't need a manual to tell us what page to turn to, because we have a wealth of expertise and experience from which to draw, and draw from it we will. If we want our students to embrace their struggles, then we must embrace ours with the same enthusiasm. After all, as I have said many times to my little friends, "If you never needed help with anything and passed every test with flying colors, I wouldn't have a job."

Avoiding the Shame Spiral That Is Incessant Test Prep

Preparing for standardized testing somehow morphed into a beast that seems to have taken over all authentic teaching. Many of us teachers are mandated to do endless test preparation programs, while other teachers are so fearful for their jobs that they feel they have no other choice. And there is no joy in test prep. None. Further, this climate of endless testing also seems to ignore our true purpose and responsibility as teachers of reading, which is to create lifelong readers who live active reading lives. Yet, tragically, so many schools waste precious school hours by championing these relentless testing tactics and simply hoping that students pick up a love of reading along the way. As a result, I have seen too many teachers fall down the shame spiral of test prep. Implementing rote test prep drills is not the stuff of our teacher dreams, nor do we fundamentally believe that this is a good use of our students' instructional time, *but* we also feel the intense pressure to prepare our students for the intensity of the tests they will face, and worry that if we don't drill them, they may not really be ready.

Beyond our obligation as teachers of reading, several studies have concluded that there is a strong correlation between the amount of time students spend reading and their performance on standardized reading tests (Gallagher, 2009). In addition, a fairly recent study supports that reading for pleasure is highly linked to college attendance and a managerial or professional job later in life (University of Oxford, as cited by Miller, 2014).

Are you not yet convinced that test prep is not only painful but also crazily effective? Well, then, I have a story for you—a horror story of sorts.

Eight teachers from the second- and third-grade teams sat around a table in an empty classroom after the children had been dismissed, discussing the third grade's crushing test prep. The conversation went something like this:

Third-grade super colleague:	So, the amount of test prep we have to do is overwhelming. We don't get to start teaching science or social studies until April! We were thinking some of it could start in second grade.
Me:	[mouth gaping open] Um, OK. Although that's a little horrifying to think about, I guess I understand. Your hands are tied because the test prep is all mandated.
Third-grade super colleague:	Look, I know it's insane, but we need help so maybe we can spend more time actually teaching and less time prepping.
Me:	I think I might be crying. Am I crying?
Third-grade super colleague:	A little.

I am not sure if it is more horrifying that third-grade teachers feel that there is no time to teach science and social studies (where so much reading and writing come together while simultaneously building students' background knowledge, which in turn heightens their ability to comprehend text—basically, a circle of amazing!) until the spring or that there are teachers considering beginning formal test prep in second grade. Both realities keep me awake at night when I think about the happiness of my favorite teachers, the happiness of students, and the happiness of my own small fries as they prepare to enter school themselves.

Test prep should not dominate your reading instruction. When test prep dominates classroom life and becomes the mainstay of our reading instruction, we are creating a very narrow vision of what it means to be a reader for our students. In the wise words of Donalyn Miller (2014), "Our zealous national focus on standardized test performance, often at the expense of meaningful reading instruction and support, has caused us to lose sight of our true obligations regarding children's literacy: fostering their capacity to lead literate lives" (p. xx). Formal test prep should be taught for maybe a week or two prior to the test. Period. Full stop. We need to familiarize our students with the various types of questions they may encounter, but beyond that, more time to engage with authentic reading material and receive targeted instruction is what students need. It would be irresponsible to not prepare our students to take the test. They need to be familiar with the academic language they may encounter, practice close reading strategies, and learn to carefully examine questions. However, it is more irresponsible to limit students' reading instruction and lives to this finite group of skills.

If Miller and I aren't enough, though, would you listen to Dr. Seuss (1998)? In his posthumous book, *Hooray for Diffendoofer Day!*, the wise doctor compares two schools as they prepare to take a very important test. One school is filled with children drawn in bright colors who love to learn from and with one another. The other school is filled with gray, uniformed children who complete worksheets and other assorted drill-and-kill exercises. The school filled with sunlight and rainbows is apprehensive as the test approaches because they have never numbed their brains with activities of that nature. But, lo and behold, they rock the test, whereas the sad little gray boys and girls do not fare so well. I say you should try restricting your test preparation to a genre study, freeing you up to do more authentic teaching and reading. Tell me that doesn't make you feel like a happier, more successful teacher working in a Seussified classroom filled with rainbows and joy.

Integrating Useful Formal Reading Assessments

As teachers of reading, we need to listen to our little friends read and discuss their authentic reading if we want to get a sense of where they are in their development as readers. If you want to use meaningful assessments as a way to remember that it is important to pause and celebrate success as well as plan an optimistic future, incorporate a running record into your reading instruction. It is time to get on the bandwagon. Formal running records allow you to listen carefully to your students as they read and to discuss their reading, and provide us with a benchmark to look at our class (or a grade level) as a whole. Do not fall for the temptation to let someone else complete your running records. I know these assessments can be tedious and time-consuming, but they are valuable tools, and nothing can replace the experience of listening to your students read and respond in this sort of formal testing scenario.

So, what can you do to avoid the piles, mess, and disorganization that seem to come along with administering a running record to your entire class? The following tips have not only been used by me, but I have also combed through resources from some of the greats to compile these ideas. This stuff is golden.

Preparation

Begin by double-checking the level at which your students left off last year or at the last administration to avoid fishing around for the right level or wasting your time repeating an unnecessary level. Make a list of your students. (You knew *that* was coming, right? There is literally no occasion for which I cannot think of an appropriate list.) After each student's name, write the level that he or she last passed successfully and leave space to record the level passed successfully during this administration and space for any notes that may occur to you, such as where you left off in your testing. Now, take your list and prepare your materials: Photocopy the appropriate blackline masters, fill in the name and date type of information, and pull all the correct texts. Organize your materials in the order that you plan on testing your kids. (Hint: Don't save your most challenging students for last. It will be a total buzzkill. Spread the wealth so you don't end up totally backed up at the end of a long week of assessing.)

Administration

Preparation of this sort should not be taken lightly. Diving in is a mess. Although I admire your just-go-for-it spirit, it is not worth the drama on the back end when you find yourself encased in a mountain of piles and not sure where you left off. Give yourself a few days to get it together. I speak from experience when I tell you that giving yourself the mental space to prepare and the physical time to gather and organize does wonders for your sense of happiness and overall Zen. It also means a strong commitment to planning and knowing where you are going with instruction beyond just the next day.

I learned this the hard way in my first year of teaching. I knew I had to begin administering running records on Monday, so Friday at lunch, I headed down to the photocopier to get myself all set up. I thought 30 minutes was more than enough time to copy 25 short packets. Now I look back at that moment and laugh at my sillier, younger self—so naive! I laugh because it keeps me from crying. I had no idea that my degree from a four-year institution and my Ivy League master's degree did not qualify me to press the numbers and then hit the big green "Print" button. I mean, I was trusted with the minds of 20 young people, but the photocopier? Now *that* is important and should be cherished. Long story short, I had to fill out several requests to copy my materials, have my requests authorized by an administrator (perhaps because they thought I would use the copier questionably?), and then submit said requests to the proper chosen one who was allowed to touch the buttons. I did all this insanity only to be told that they were "backed up" and would not be able to fulfill my request until Thursday of the following week. Cut to me walking to Staples to copy my materials at my own cost. The lesson of all this? Do not allow the preparation for assessment get the better of you.

But back to the issue at hand, formal running records. When it comes to the actual administration of a running record, try to stagger students so you are listening to one student read and then sending him or her off to complete the text while you get another student started. There is no need to hold conferences or small groups during the week you plan on completing your running records; after all, this *is* conference work and crucial to directing your work moving forward. One key element to your happiness as a reading teacher is to remember to take a breath every once in a while and not try to cram in everything every single day—quality over quantity, my friends.

I don't know about you, but when I am giving a student a running record, my mind is racing as I listen. I hear all sorts of mistakes and areas for improvement; it's almost like it's raining goals. (Isn't that a song? It's raining goals, hallelujah, it's raining goals! Yeaaaa!) I dutifully record everything on the official testing sheet but also like to have these observations and ideas in a separate place in my own words. So, I always have a set of index cards handy when I'm giving running records. I jot down everything that occurs to me as I listen to a student read and respond. Then, before I move on to the next student (remember, take a moment to breathe), I look closely at my results, do a quick miscue analysis, and think about specific comprehension goals. This all gets noted on my index cards. Later, at the end of the week when all the running records have been completed, I take my trusty index cards home and review my notes. I use these to plan my future instruction with each child and to see patterns for possible small groups. Key to my own professional happiness is not feeling overwhelmed by a barrage of reading goals for each student. When I write them down, I am able to thoughtfully select the one or two most pressing goals and systematically think about how I am going to address them with the particular student or small group. Once I feel that goal has been achieved, I turn back to my index cards, consider my more recent observations of that student in action, and select where I would like to go next. It feels more sane than trying to address five goals at the same time, and it is clearer for the student. (We will get down and dirty with goal setting in Chapter 6.)

Combining Formal Assessments With Informal Data

The all-knowing and fabulous Debbie Diller (2007) uses a great analogy to describe the importance of combining formal and informal data when making instructional decisions for students: When we go to the doctor and present what is ailing us, we want the doctor to combine research-based medical knowledge with our observations to choose the best treatment plan. Likewise, context, observation, and real-time authentic work often color and add texture to our understanding of students' needs. Long story short, we know our students as readers. We have a sense of their struggles and observe their independent reading habits. Our observations of students as they read authentically are just as important as formal data when making decisions for students.

Now, all of that formal data is lovely and can be very informative, but of equal value is the informal data gathered from your informal observations of students. Yes, this is legit data, particularly if you are recording your observations (as you should, because how can you remember anything after a long day?!). Read with your students. Listen to your students read. Talk with your students about books. Notice their book choices. Find out more about their individual preferences as readers and how they feel about reading. Then, write it all down. (I encourage you to use color-coded pens and index cards or your personal office supply of choice. Don't underestimate the joy to be found in the perfect pen or notebook.) In short, get to know them as readers. Don't be afraid to share who you are as a reader with them as well. Perhaps some of you have never considered your own preferences or reading identity before. Do it now. This is what it is all about: connecting with students about their reading lives and pushing them gently to expand their preferences, overcome obstacles, tackle new genres, or find more space in their lives for consuming text for pleasure.

I have been told by many teachers that they feel pressure to constantly be engaged with a student for fear that an administrator might pop in and catch them not working with at least one student. OK, first of all, this is insane. We are professionals, yet we talk about people catching us doing things? Granted, if you're surfing Facebook on your smartphone in the middle of reading, you deserve to get caught, and get caught you will. But if you are taking a step back to observe the progress and working rhythms of your class, isn't that part of your job, to monitor your students as you prepare them to be independent workers and thinkers who don't need to have their hands held at every moment of the day? Being a professional kid watcher is a key responsibility of teachers and something that brought me a great deal of joy in my own practice. To start with, it meant another stack of color-coded index cards, and that alone is enough to bring a smile to my face. It also meant seeking out moments of independence to highlight and celebrate, catching snippets of conversations that give greater insight into student understanding, and discovering more about their largely hilarious personalities. My students were always the most amazingly funny when they thought I wasn't looking.

Taking the Temperature of the Room

All of this one-on-one testing nonsense is lovely and productive, and although I'm sure you are smiling from ear to ear, sometimes a girl has to get a sense of the general group. Are we lost in the sauce, or can I move on? Sometimes you need a quick way to take everyone's temperature without a huge formal, time-consuming assessment. The danger here is assigning students some massive task that pulls them away from their reading time. Keep it quick and informative. As is everything in teaching, this is easier said than done.

Look critically at your unit of study. What are the key pieces of learning that you want all students to walk away with? What are the goals of your unit, and where are they reflected most obviously in your teaching during that unit? Where are the natural stopping points where it is crucial that everyone be on board before moving on? Once you identify those points (and I would caution you to only look for three or four moments to avoid chopping up your flow), think carefully about what sort of information you need. Do you really need that intense graphic organizer? Are students more focused on filling out the sheet and completing the task than they are engaged in something authentic that truly reflects their current level of understanding? I have been guilty of handing out an extensive organizer that includes a complex matrix of items for students to fill out, which renders my formative assessment somewhat tedious as well as time-consuming.

I like to compare a good formative assessment with Coco Chanel's notion of a chic outfit. She says you should get dressed in the morning, look in the mirror, and then take off the last thing you put on. What she was saying was that people often overdo it when getting dressed to go out, and I think the same can be said of a well-designed formative assessment. Create your assessment. Then, look at it with an editorial eye and remove something.

Everything doesn't have to be so serious and wrought with effort. Keep it light. Keep it purposeful. How do you tighten up your informal formative assessments? Ask students to produce something very quick, informal, and in the moment. Use their initials rather than their full names. Pass out half sheets of paper, sticky notes, or index cards that feel less intimidating than a sheet of lined paper. Allow students to record their thinking in bulleted points (when appropriate). Will a drawing suffice or a word or two? Remember, you need to look through all of these papers in a timely manner, and you know as well as I do that dragging home a teacher bag full of unfinished work will suck the joy right out of your day and probably give you some sort of back issue. What's worse is when you realize that there is no time to look at those papers tonight, you drag them right back to school the next day, and they mock you the entire way.

If You're Assessing and You Know It, Clap Your Hands!

I think a key point to remember when deciding which assessments deserve your time and energy is this: If you are not going to look carefully at the data and use it to immediately help you shape your instruction, it's not worth sweating. Do it because you probably have to, but don't let it get to you. Let it reside in the same place as cleaning out the litter box and having your taxes done. Instead, focus your time and energy on those assessments that breathe new life into your instruction. Keep their delivery light and purposeful. Our kids pick up what we are putting down, and if we need a little fake it 'til we make it, then there you go.

CHAPTER 5

Let's Get Together

How to Collaborate With Colleagues

> *I had come to understand one critical fact about my happiness project: I couldn't change anyone else.*
>
> —Gretchen Rubin (2011, p. 40)

Schools attract all kinds of people. While working in schools, I have met some of the most amazing, wonderful, and genuine friends I will ever have. I have met some of the most impressive, hardworking, brilliant colleagues in schools, but I have also met some of the most bizarre and ineffective people, too. In a single school day, my colleagues have the ability to make me laugh, improve my practice, ease the load of teaching, and also make me want to punch myself in the face. All too often, I let difficult colleagues ruin my day when really I should have treated them like that annoyingly short crayon with no paper that lurks in the corner of every box. I know this is nothing unique; everyone in every profession everywhere has to work with particularly difficult colleagues, but somehow, when you work with children in a school, it all seems much more dire.

Poor collegial relationships are a key source of workplace-related stress for teachers (Brown & Ralph, 1998). However, successful relationships between teachers have a hand in shaping their beliefs, values, and habits and improving their general sense of work satisfaction, level of productivity, and feelings of effectiveness (Firestone & Pennell, 1993; Hargreaves, 1994). In other words, we are not all playing nicely in the sandbox. And when we don't play nicely with one another, we are making our daily work lives much more difficult, much less effective, and much less happy.

Just like in previous chapters, I want to share with you the roadblocks I put up to achieving happiness as a teacher. I will be the first one to admit that I spent too much time worrying about what everyone else was doing and gossiping about. We are better than that! First, let's chat about some of the stress factors that can result from working with the difficult, not-so-super colleagues, and then I will offer some tips on how to prevent that stress—or at least control how those colleagues affect you so you can prevent your interactions with them from casting a dark shadow on your teacher happiness. Then, I will explore the healthy, happy results that can be produced by spending time and energy with those who deserve it and who can also help us become better teachers—our super colleagues.

Recognizing Super and Not-So-Super Colleagues

To recapture our happiness, it is essential to differentiate clearly between those who are super colleagues and those who are just bringing us down. We all know what super colleagues look like. These are the teachers who run a classroom that you secretly want to sit in the back of all day so you can take notes on all the fabulousness. These teachers ground their work in best practices yet, at the same time, are unafraid to try something new or to learn from others. They enjoy collaborating. They are happy to squeeze in a quick working lunch, to meet after school, or to do what it takes to best meet the needs of their students. A true super colleague is not a know-it-all or out to make anyone else look bad. Instead, his or her confidence and dedication are contagious and inspiring.

However, the reality is that most of us also find ourselves forced to work with colleagues who are not so super. According to literature on stress and teachers, working with challenging colleagues is a very common stressor that impacts teachers' sense of job satisfaction (Brown & Ralph, 1998; Carlyle & Woods, 2002; Firestone & Pennell, 1993; Travers & Cooper, 1998). Translation? You are bound to work with people who bring you down and disrupt your teacher Zen. But what is it exactly about those colleagues that disrupts our happiness? We are professionals and adults after all, so it has to be more than just "they bug me."

I don't know what strikes you most as being a cause for the stressful relationships you might have with some of your colleagues, but some other factors cited in the research on stress and teaching include personality clashes, poor systems of communication, lack of community spirit, little social or academic interaction among various staff groupings, and an uneven distribution of workloads (Brown & Ralph, 1998). For me, it was the uneven distribution of workloads that was the most infuriating factor. One year, my school organized curricular committees to work toward increased horizontal and vertical alignment across each major area of instruction. Each and every week, as classroom teachers met after a long day of working with their students to discuss, research, and realign units of study, I watched one of the teachers on my committee use that time to continually text and nap. Yes, that's right, nap! Then, when we asked this teacher to do some copying between meetings so the teacher could, you know, *contribute*, he cited his schedule as prohibitive to getting this done, despite having at least three free periods each and every day! (Are you starting to feel the negative energy? Very un-Zen but, sadly, true.)

How to Stay Fabulous When Working With the Good, the Bad, and the Rest

Taking Control of the Stress Caused by Challenging Colleagues

For many years, I spent a tremendous amount of my professional time and effort trying to make it known how hard I was working in comparison with others who seemed to only take their lunches seriously. I needed my principal to notice how much more effort and thought I put into my day. It was almost as if I wanted a gold star or a happy face on my behavior chart. In other words, I was acting a little childish. It was like I couldn't help myself; I needed to differentiate myself and have my hard work acknowledged or at least distinguished from the laziness I observed in some of my colleagues. But then I started to ask myself, Who am I to point out the shortcomings of other staff members or draw attention to my own hard work in a needy, look-at-me fashion? Whether we like it or not, teachers do not have the ability or power to evaluate or dismiss colleagues deemed ineffective.

Then, I read something profound in *The Happiness Project: Or, Why I Spent a Year Trying to Sing in the Morning, Clean My Closets, Fight Right, Read Aristotle, and Generally Have More Fun* (Rubin, 2011). (See? I am trying hard to move into a happier, more positive space.) Rubin says,

"Why did I have such a need for gold stars? Was it vanity that needed to be stoked? Was it insecurity that needed to be soothed?...So I made the resolution 'Don't expect praise or appreciation'" (pp. 44–45). She continues by recognizing that she did certain things to make herself happy, not for the acknowledgment of others. It was like I had been hit by a ton of bricks. This made sense! I spend Sundays planning because it makes *me* feel happy and sane. It doesn't matter how others spend their Sundays or if they spend as much time planning. I collaborate with my colleagues to tweak our units of study because *I* find it invigorating, not because I need to make other, less engaged staff members look bad. I spend time reading children's literature because *I* genuinely enjoy it and love discussing it with my students, not so I can point out someone who routinely discusses books with her students that she has never read. Although I know I do many of these things for my students (because it is really all about the kids), thinking about how my own choices about hard work were wrapped up in what makes *me* happy and what makes *me* feel like the best teacher I can be helped diffuse my frustration with less effective staff. If this sounds familiar at all, then take my advice: Stop setting yourself up for disappointment and frustration. Spend less time noticing and cataloguing how little these individuals contribute, and instead focus on how your choices about your work make *you* feel effective and happy.

Have you had enough of my two cents? Let's take a closer look at the research on teacher stress for some solutions. What do the experts say about playing nicely in the sandbox? I dug up three clear, problem-focused strategies for us to chat about: changing the situation, changing your expectations, and making the problem less important or central to your well-being (Walsh, 1998). These all sound lovely, don't they? But what do they actually look like?

To me, it seems that if you choose to change the situation, you need to change how, when, and why you interact with these individuals. A less intense version of this might mean carefully choosing only like-minded or equally hardworking colleagues with whom to collaborate. A more intense route to changing the situation might be sitting down and having a frank conversation with these colleagues, allowing them to also speak to the situation at hand. Of course, this type of conversation needs to be handled respectfully and professionally, but it could be a key step toward mutual understanding and a shift in your current working relationship.

If changing the situation feels a bit much for you, consider changing your expectations. In the scenario that I described earlier in the chapter about the noncontributing teacher on my curricular committee, I decided not to expect that teacher to contribute in any meaningful way or to respond to our invitations to join in on conversations. That teacher had self-selected out of our work, and there was nothing I could do to change that. The moral of the story: Stop setting yourself up for disappointment.

One final way to regain control over your feelings about these relationships (because you will never control the work ethic of these individuals) is to make the problem less important to your daily routine. For example, if the speech teacher who is supposed to push into your classroom and work one on one with students never shows up on time, stop integrating his or her presence into your routine. If that teacher enters the room 20 minutes late and you have already begun to line up for lunch, so be it. My blood would boil in situations like this until I realized that I was not the one who was late or slacking off in my responsibilities, so I was not the one who should be uncomfortable in the situation. To keep control over my feelings, I had to come up with a mantra to deal with this situation, repeat that mantra in my head over and over until it felt comfortable, and then use it each time this situation arose: "I am so sorry, but you are 20 minutes late, and we had to move on with our day." To the colleague who refused to meet at times that were not mandated by the school, "You and I just have different styles of working, but I can't wait until our next staff meeting to think about how I am going to address this student's needs." To the colleague who expected us to recap the last five meetings that he or she chose not to attend because we voluntarily met during our lunch, "I wish you had come to all the meetings we invited you to, but right now repeating everything we have already discussed is not a good use of our time."

I let the stress of my relationships with ineffective colleagues dominate my mood for too long. I was angry, frustrated, and determined to either make them work as hard as me and my super colleagues or demonstrate to the administration how little these people contributed to the students. Maybe you feel the same way from time to time. This took my time and focus away from my teaching, and once I realized that, I knew it was time for me to change. We can still dish out the occasional snarky comment to a friend, but complaining alone will not change anything and will leave us still feeling fairly agitated. Take back control of these relationships, or at least control how much time and emotional energy you allow them to have, and tell me if you don't feel better.

Relying on Super Colleagues to Lighten Your Load

OK, enough about *those* colleagues. I make sure that the not-so-super colleagues don't overshadow the amazing work and contributions of my super colleagues in my professional life, and we won't let them overshadow the potential of these relationships here either. Teacher job satisfaction and happiness are tightly tied to positive working relationships (Carlyle & Woods, 2002), so these are the relationships that should command more of your time and attention.

Some of my closest personal friends are the women with whom I teach. Everything about these relationships makes my life as a teacher better and happier—from lurking in one of their doorways on a Friday morning to discuss what we plan to do that evening, to celebrating one another's birthdays in a 10-minute choke-down-this-cupcake-because-we-love-you-but-need-to-hit-the-copier-before-picking-up-our-class party, to choosing to stay after school to work on creating exciting new reading lessons for our students.

Part of owning your own fabulousness is recognizing fabulousness in others and choosing to spend your time—both personal and professional—with colleagues who will hold you up, close the door to listen to you vent after a tough day, or simply dish on the latest episode of your favorite show. As teachers, we need people who will be in our corner, who will watch our class when we really need to go to the bathroom, and who will be there when our personal lives make our professional lives hard.

One year, I was in the airport on my way home from a long weekend away when I got a phone call from one of my super colleagues, who is also one of my good friends. She had had a profoundly sad and shocking family emergency happen over the weekend and was going to be out of school for an indefinite amount of time. She was unable to reach our principal and was not going to be able to put together plans. However, in the midst of this tragedy, she called me because she was worried about how this would all impact her students and her progress with them as readers. I spent the plane ride making lists (of course) of whom to call and what needed to be done. When I got home, I got in touch with the administration and told them what was going on. I called my other super colleagues, and we all sprang into action. For the next four weeks, we planned all of our colleague's reading lessons, conferences, and small groups. We created a schedule with the help of our reading coach so we could rotate in and out of her room to actually teach reading to her students, rather than asking the substitute to do it. We split up her class to welcome them into ours during read-alouds. We sent her e-mails reassuring her that everyone was fine and not behind at all. I am not telling this story to toot my own horn; I am telling this story because I know that in every school, there are groups of super colleagues doing similar things for one another. I have never had another career, so I don't know if this happens outside the world of education, but I know that my colleagues have helped me through some of the most challenging personal and professional times of my life. That is something to feel grateful for, to cultivate and nurture, and to feel happy about.

Beyond this, super colleagues can and should come together to help ease the intensity of a reading teacher's workload and to push one another professionally. An overwhelming workload and demands on a teacher's time are also cited as sources of workplaces stress and things that make you feel less than Zen (Brown & Ralph, 1998; Valli & Buese, 2007). Teaching reading is no joke. There are a million things to know, a million parts to manage, and a million things to learn to improve your practice. Never try to be an island. While I am sure you are fabulous all on your own, you are far more fabulous when you join forces with your super colleagues to share the workload together. Of course, this can only happen after you build the appropriate amount of trust in one another's work. No one wants to share phenomenal ideas for lessons only to receive a screwy photocopy of a worksheet in return. Once you have found colleagues whom you trust and admire, it is game on.

Planning Together. My Sunday planning brunches were always a solitary activity because it was a time when I laid out how I was going to logistically manage all the moving parts in my own room. But when it came to thinking about the content of those lessons or how I was going to reach the goals I had set for a particular small group, I always preferred to work alongside my super colleagues. There was something thrilling and wonderfully nerdy about sitting together after school discussing our reading instruction—planning new lessons, tweaking old strategies, and sharing new ideas for texts. I always walked away from those planning sessions feeling as if we had accomplished a tremendous amount and as if my personal load had been lightened.

In advance of beginning the next reading unit on our calendar, my super colleagues and I would find a time to meet. Sometimes it was for an hour, and other times it was for 15 minutes. During that time, we would take a look at the resources required for teaching that unit and put together a plan for gathering or sharing any necessary items. From time to time, we would also bring new resources to the table to consider and share with one another. We would take time to reflect on the teaching of that unit from the year before: What are the broad goals of the unit? What went well? What felt less effective? What were the predictable problems we knew our students were likely to encounter? How could we plan to teach into those problems or misunderstandings? Depending on our level of comfort with the unit at hand and the answers to these questions, this part of our conversation could span more than one meeting. Finally, we reviewed what we asked students to do as readers during this unit of study. Were they required to do any sort of writing or produce something to reflect their learning? We would debate the merits of this product, making any necessary modifications in light of our primary goal, which was always to provide students with as much independent reading time in books of their choosing as possible.

Discussing Students. We are not saints. Many times, it was more like venting about students, but I also relied on my super colleagues to discuss the struggles that my students encountered as readers and to strategize what could be done to deal with these struggles. It is critical to never think you have all the answers; more often than not, you have a super colleague who has tried something in a similar situation that you would have never thought of and it is genius. Without the confidence and mutual trust to admit when we are unsure of how to proceed, we will never grow as teachers, and we will continue to be bogged down by the struggles of our students. That does not a happy teacher make.

These exchanges do not have to be formally scheduled. Often, it is impossible to schedule them because struggles pop up out of the blue at unpredictable times and need to be dealt with in a timely fashion. More likely, one of us would pop into another super colleague's classroom with a set of conference notes and say, "I can't figure out how to improve this student's fluency. Take a look at my notes. What have you tried?" These conversations were the most productive when they were grounded in the needs of the student and punctuated by actual student work. Try sitting together and doing a miscue analysis with the running records of your most challenging students. Think about bringing your small-group notes to a colleague and asking for his or her thoughts about how to move forward. Sometimes the conversation is enough to get you unstuck and feeling positive about the work once again.

An important part of discussing your students with your super colleagues is knowing whom to go to with what. What are your super colleagues famous for? What do they know a lot about? Perhaps you know that one of your colleagues encountered a similar problem last year and may have some sage advice. Perhaps you know that another colleague loves mysteries and would be able to share some titles for you to recommend to a student who also loves mysteries. Maybe another colleague has done a lot of research on reading comprehension or reader's notebooks and can offer some ideas. Equally important, though, is becoming famous for knowing a lot about something yourself. What area of reading instruction do you find the most intriguing or exciting? Take it upon yourself to learn about that area. Learning something new feels good. Expanding your skill set as a teacher of reading feels good. Being famous for something feels good. Feeling valued and contributing in meaningful ways to the work of your colleagues feels good. It's another win–win.

Sharing Resources. Whenever I work with a group of teachers, I try to bring a new read-aloud that I hope they have never heard before. Teachers may love booklists more than any other resource on the planet. If you mention a good booklist in a room full of teachers, you will see heads snap around in anticipation like someone has just thrown a handful of 100-dollar bills into the air. I find that incredibly nerdy and awesome all at the same time. In reality, most of us are basically hoarders. We hoard booklists, we hoard ideas for teaching difficult strategies, and we hoard samples of outstanding student work. One of the things I love most about teachers is our willingness to share these resources with others; true super colleagues never hoard solely for their own benefit.

You had to know that I was going to suggest some sort of list making as key to your professional happiness, right? There is little in life that can't be made better with a good list, in my opinion. When I am feeling stressed or overwhelmed at home, my husband has learned that all it takes to cheer me up is to just push a pad of my favorite list-making paper and a good pen in my direction. (Is that sad?) So, of course, I am going to suggest that you curate and share lists of titles with one another. Whether it is titles that work well for a particular genre study, titles that work well for tackling a particular strategy, close readings that are meaty while sustaining student interest, titles to suggest to students, or titles for juicy read-alouds, make the lists, save the lists, share the lists.

However, I also want to push you and your super colleagues one step further because although lists of books are in and of themselves a beautiful thing, they can also feel intimidating because now you have to theoretically *read* these titles to effectively incorporate them into your practice. As teachers of reading, clearly we love to read ourselves. However, there are only so many hours in the day. (And, if you teach a lower grade, there only so many Magic Tree House books you can read before crying uncle. They are wonderful, but you know what I mean. Sometimes you just need to curl up with a *People* magazine.) So, put together a plan for tackling several of these texts with the help of your super colleagues. Periodically throughout the school year, my super colleagues and I would divvy up a list of texts to read and report back on. Each of us would read our assigned title(s) and write up a quick cheat sheet about the book(s). In advance, we agreed on the type of information to include on this cheat sheet: title, author, synopsis, themes, sections for close readings, and so forth. We were careful to keep these cheat sheets short, purposeful, and not uber time-consuming. (Again, *People* magazine is calling.) After exchanging these cheat sheets, I always felt lighter and more prepared to integrate fresh new works of literature into my classroom.

Learning Together. As teachers, we need to practice a bit of what we preach, and embrace new learning. Every teacher can find ways to refine and refresh his or her practice with new ideas, and moreover, resisting positive change and the integration of new techniques can be exhausting. Although it is essential to stay true to your beliefs and knowledge of best practices, it is equally essential to your own happiness to continue to grow. Research supports this by citing opportunities to learn as a key to job satisfaction (Beijaard, Meijer, & Verloop, 2004; Valli & Buese, 2007). But let's be real: Although some of us have access to amazing professional development resources, some of us have to make our own opportunities.

So, how do you do that? Gather a group of super colleagues for a professional book club. Select a book, read and discuss it together, and then commit to trying some of your new learning right away. This piece is important! Think about finding times or working with administrators to coordinate observing one another. Reflect on how it went and then rinse and repeat. Today, however, we are fortunate to have a variety of ways to learn professionally on our own. You and your super colleagues might wish to turn to social media. (Twitter, Pinterest, and Facebook all have wonderful learning opportunities if you scroll past posts and pictures of what people ate for dinner last night.) You may also wish to check out free offerings for webinars sponsored by publishers like Scholastic or professional organizations like the International Reading Association.

Finally, work with your super colleagues to learn more about the possibility of integrating technology into your daily routines. Don't roll your eyes; the technology train is here, and our students are intrigued by it and already using it, so we might as well jump on board. Plus, there are a lot of fabulous ways that technology can pump up the volume on what we are already doing. Students can research background knowledge on a time period, an author, or a certain subject to help aid in their comprehension of a new text. Students can share their reading lives and learning with one another in ways that feel much more authentic than a (gag) book report. Students can view and create book trailers that get them excited about their reading and thinking about what book might come next for them. You can keep and organize conference and small-group notes without ever needing to go to the photocopier, because there's an app for that! You can integrate video clips, slideshows, or digital presentations into your instruction and to serve as a resource for students at home. You can keep families up to date on the work happening in your classroom and how they might support their children as readers. Yes, there are all of these wonderful things you can do, but for many of us, until we experiment with them and talk through them with our colleagues, we don't feel ready to integrate them into our practice.

Just Do It

Teaching reading effectively takes a tremendous amount of knowledge, effort, and time. This means that we no longer have time to focus on the stressful relationships that we may have with those not-so-super colleagues. Instead, we have to focus on the positive contributions of our super colleagues and their ability to provide emotional support, ease our workloads, and enhance our daily instruction. Perhaps reading the suggestions in this chapter feels intimidating, unrealistic, or like I work every waking moment. Quite the opposite. If I did not collaborate with and rely on my colleagues in this way, all of this work would have fallen squarely on my shoulders. And there is no way that I would be able to keep up. I mean, I already never make it to the gym as it is, but to accomplish all of this on my own, I might have to give up sleeping—not to mention that working collaboratively always felt invigorating and was punctuated with talk of our lives and so much laughter. Working with my super colleagues always made the impossible pieces of teaching reading feel more possible.

Research on teacher collaboration supports the idea that having a successful working relationship with your colleagues not only reduces work-related stress levels but also accounts for increased feelings of teaching efficacy (Carlyle & Woods, 2002; Datnow, 2011; Hargreaves, 1994). Who doesn't like to feel more effective and less strung out? However, research also tells us that there are two types of teacher collaboration: the amazing makes-you-want-to-click-your-heels-together-in-midair kind and the more forced or contrived kind. There may be nothing you can do about being a part of contrived efforts at collaboration; I know we all often feel like we are obligated to attend meeting after meeting after meeting in which nothing meaningful is accomplished. These failed attempts at fostering a collaborative environment are often mandated in a top-down fashion, have rigid goals determined by individuals outside the classroom, and occur at particular places at particular times (Hargreaves, 1994). I mean, at the end of the day, all I can say to you is that you just have to go to these meetings. The silver lining is that in some cases, these more prescriptive meetings can lead to or inspire more authentic collaborative moments (Datnow, 2011). When these predetermined meetings do not come with a tightly defined agenda, teachers can use this space and time provided by the administration to work in authentic ways about the matter at hand

(Lieberman & Miller, 2008). Moreover, by attending these meetings, you can determine who might be the most open to participating in more spontaneous, authentic collaborative endeavors.

So, what do we know about true, authentic teacher collaboration? I'm so glad you asked! According to Hargreaves's (1994) seminal work on teacher collaboration, a truly collaborative school culture consists of teachers who voluntarily initiate tasks and purposes for working together. Although the administration may support and facilitate these meetings, they are sustained by motivation from the teaching community, not top-down demands. Therefore, true collaborative efforts may occur during scheduled meeting times, but scheduling does not dominate the conversation. Teachers are most likely to sustain this work when there is a shared belief that working together is not only productive but enjoyable as well. Finally, the outcomes of collaboration are unpredictable and change over time. Teachers may develop a new series of lessons, collaborate to analyze student data, or discuss instructional methods—each of which yields a very different product.

I know many of you out there want desperately to collaborate with your colleagues in meaningful ways but struggle to find the time. I have also talked with teachers who are afraid to meet during common free periods or lunch for fear of being ostracized by other teachers who are less inclined to do this because of union-related issues. However, remember that we teachers have the right to voluntarily decide to meet and do amazing work whenever we can and want to.

Although we can't change who we work with, we can take back control of how and with whom we spend the majority of our time, effort, and energy. Nurture your positive relationships with fellow super colleagues. Send one another love notes. Buy one another treats for no reason (chocolates can do wonders on a tough day). Find the time to meet. Take the time to get to know one another outside of your lives at school. Laugh about the antics of your students because they are funny. Not all of our schools will be an oasis of positive working relationships, but we have the ability to create pockets of collaboration that are authentic, help improve our practices as teachers of reading, and make us—wait for it—happy.

CHAPTER 6

Let's Get in the Zone

Improving Your Teacher Stamina During the Literacy Block Marathon

> Research has shown that teachers who plan with regard to students'
> abilities and needs and who are flexible while teaching are more
> effective, especially at stimulating higher-order thinking, than
> teachers who engage in extensive preplanning that is tightly focused
> on behavioral objectives and coverage of facts.
>
> —Linda Darling-Hammond (1997, p. 72)

Picture it: It's time for reading. A classroom teacher whirls around the classroom at a frenetic pace. She begins with her students on the rug. After a quick minilesson, the students go back to their seats, and the teacher glances at the clock. Ticktock, ticktock. She grabs a clipboard and a pen and walks with purpose to meet with a student. She glances at the clock. She moves to the next student. She glances at the clock. There is a hint of desperation around her eyes, and you can see her grow slightly distracted in her work with the student as she starts to shuffle her notes around. After another glance at the clock, she jogs to the back table and grabs a stack of books, calling over a group of students. She looks at the clock again. She meets with her first group but is noticeably more distracted as she tries to listen to each student, jot down a few notes, and put out fires around the classroom from her current vantage point: "No, you may not go to the bathroom." "Please sit down." "Yes, you should have brought your book with you to the back table." Before the first group has even left their chairs, she is calling over the next group, asking them to move quickly and get settled. There goes the clock again. Ticktock, ticktock.

Does this sound familiar? Exhausting? Teaching reading effectively means managing a tremendous number of moving parts without routinely sweating through your clothes or curling up in the corner until someone brings you a coffee. (More coffee, please!) Teaching a tight literacy block can feel like an endurance challenge. Wait, it *is* an endurance challenge, and just like any athlete, teachers need time and space to build up their stamina and perfect their making-it-look-easy joie-de-teaching style.

I am a devoted reader of Gretchen Rubin's blog, The Happiness Project (www.gretchenrubin.com). Sometimes I integrate her teachings into my life, and other times I just fantasize about how fabulous I might be someday when I have a chance to feng shui my life. Like a true teacher, I am able to relate just about everything back to teaching, and many of her wise words have found their way into my classroom. She rocked my world with her discussion about the detriments of multitasking, which is actually counterproductive and can contribute to feelings of stress and unhappiness. You end up feeling as if you did a little bit of everything poorly and nothing completely or well. I can't tell you how many times I found myself running around my classroom checking in with one student while trying to finish up conference notes on another, keeping a watchful eye on a small group and stopping to give another group a thumbs-up, all in the same three minutes. I probably accomplished none of my desired goals and instead looked like a panicked mess. Multitasking fails. To paraphrase the wise words of Debbie Diller (2007), I am the best model of reading in the classroom, and in those moments, am I modeling what I would like my students to emulate? No, I am modeling crazy face. There is no joy in crazy face.

So, how do we use our time wisely, maintain our sanity, hold true to our beliefs, and feel happy while doing it? In this chapter, I outline four of the basic components of a successful reading block: the minilesson, the read-aloud, the conference, and small-group instruction. These four structures may seem simple at first, but if you have tried to do it all before, you know as well as I do that it can quickly go from "I've got this in the bag" to "How am I supposed to fit everything in?" in the blink of an eye. So, in addition to a basic discussion of these components, I've included some tips on how to focus your energy and keep up your stamina as you enter your literacy block.

Let Them Read! Hang on to Your Core Beliefs About Best Practices

Students get to be better readers by reading, not by listening to us talk about reading. As I mentioned before in Chapter 3, Richard Allington (2012) cites 90 minutes as the amount of time children need to have their eyes on text in any given school day. I am coming back to this statistic not to send you into a state of panic but to reinforce the importance of this core belief: Students need time to read. Just read. Therefore, it becomes essential that we tailor all the other trappings of reading instruction to prioritize this goal. (By the by, it also means that we need to think about ways to infuse reading meaningfully across the day, but that's a topic for another book.)

In addition to allowing students time to read, we must consider the importance of allowing students to make their own choices about their reading material (Allington, 2013; Allyn, 2012; Gallagher, 2009; Miller, 2009, 2014). I know that many of you hold sacred a handful of class novels that you like to use year after year after year. Many times, these class novels are taught to the exclusion of independent reading. But imagine that you are a student in your classroom who dislikes historical fiction, or finds the book too challenging and is unable to comprehend it despite all of your conversations. I don't care about preparing for "the test"; disrupting students' ability to make choices and read independently is not acceptable and runs counter to research on best practice. I know the last thing that any of us wants is to extinguish a love of reading in a child. In *Readicide: How Schools Are Killing Reading and What You Can Do About It*, Kelly Gallagher (2009) writes, "Clearly, if we want students to perform well on standardized reading tests, our top priority should not be in narrowing students into a test-prep curriculum; our focus should be on providing our students with the widest reading experiences possible" (p. 36). Making all students read the same text to the exclusion of their own reading choices is not best practice. Not giving students adequate time to read independently because our reading instruction went longer than intended is not best practice. Talking about reading strategies without allowing students time to actually *practice* reading is not best practice. Beyond not being best practice, it makes teaching harder than it needs to be as you try to corral disengaged students.

It is all about balance. We need to strike a balance between exposing our students to a wide range of quality literature (not just our favorites) while still letting them make their own choices about reading material. We need to allow students to make their own choices while working gently with them to expand their horizons and perhaps try something new. This is where I totally have jumped on the Donalyn Miller (2009, 2014) bandwagon with the idea of genre requirements that expose students to a variety of genres and formats. Student choice doesn't mean that we are hands-off and at our desks with our feet up. It means knowing our classroom libraries well so we can guide students toward making choices that are in line with their interests and reading abilities.

Maintaining student independent reading time as sacred also means considering the types of writing that we assign to students as readers. On occasion, I have been guilty of (and have seen other teachers do as well) tasking children with writing assignments that I have no intention of looking at very carefully. It is almost like I assigned the writing so students could prove to me that they did the reading and understood it. There are three huge flaws with this thinking. First, many students are adept at fooling us. They write convincing reflections to their reading that give the impression that they are reading and comprehending the living daylights out of their books. Second, when I assign this type of writing each day, it is nearly impossible to read and respond to each entry. Therefore, I am assigning something for which I cannot provide meaningful feedback. Third, if students are spending a tremendous amount of time writing during reading, they are not really reading. Remember that whole thing about giving students uninterrupted time to just read? I'm still talking about that. It's important.

One instructional technique that has gotten a wee bit of overuse is the sticky note. Now, let's be clear. I love a good sticky note. I love sticky notes of all shapes, sizes, and colors. (One might even say that I hoard them. Don't tell!) Asking students to mark or track their thinking by placing a sticky note in their reading is a great idea. It often gives us insight into what our students are thinking (or not) as they read. However, I am in agreement with Gallagher (2009) when he cautions us to not ask students to stop and post their thinking every few paragraphs. This is extremely disruptive to their natural reading rhythms. After all, how often do you, as a real reader, stop and commemorate your personal connection to the text with a sticky note when you are curled up with a Jodi Picoult novel? I'm going to go ahead and guess that the answer is never. In addition, these sticky notes can become distracting and difficult to manage, particularly for our youngest readers and our most reluctant readers at any age. More often than not, one or two sticky notes to record a student's thoughts about the theme are sufficient, and then the student can return to the real work at hand—reading.

The Moving Parts: What Exactly Are We Trying to Accomplish?

What is it that we are trying to accomplish, you ask? Only instilling a love of reading and equipping students with the skills to engage with any reading material they choose. Seriously, I don't think many people understand the difficulties and the joys in teaching reading. We say that allowing students time to read will make them better readers, and that's true, but that certainly isn't all we have to do. Clearly, people who are not teachers (a.k.a. outsiders) say things like, "It must be nice to just read storybooks to kids all day," which makes me a bit bristly, but I don't really expect them to understand. I believe there are many teachers out there who, despite being amazing educators, also underestimate the knowledge, skill, and stamina needed to sustain your fabulousness across an entire literacy block.

Best practice teaches us that an ideal reading block contains brief, focused whole-group instruction, small-group or one-on-one teaching experiences, and independent practice time for students (Allyn, 2007, 2012; Diller, 2007; Miller, 2009). It's a lot to juggle. Feeling like the teacher I described at the beginning of this chapter is no way to spend your day because there is just no joy there. And we are crazy to think that our anxiety and tension are not projected onto our students, impacting their experience in the classroom in negative ways. Trying to jam everything in for the sake of saying you jammed it all in is a lose–lose. To have a hope of achieving any sort of Zen and creating a classroom atmosphere that welcomes and encourages joyful reading, teachers need to put in time planning and coordinating both the whole-group and the small-group experiences that they wish to tackle each day.

A teacher's ability to connect to students in meaningful ways is almost always cited as contributing to that teacher's overall sense of happiness in the classroom (Bullough, 2011; Klassen, Perry, & Frenzel, 2012; Roffey, 2012; Spilt, Koomen, & Thijs, 2011). The literacy block is an amazing opportunity to relate to your students as readers, not only to provide tailored instruction but also to feel connected to them as people. Is that too touchy-feely? It's true, though. It's story time now. Do you have a cup of coffee?

Over the years, I have had several little friends who still stand out in my mind as avid readers, as those kids who can simply not read enough. These kids read during lunch, during recess, and often while I was trying to teach something other than reading. The problem with having kids who are avid readers in your class is that sometimes they run out of books to read and are unsure of what to do next. Munchkin was one of these kids. One day he came to me and said, "I really need a new book, but I read all my favorites. Do you know a book I might like?" After choking back tears of joy, I went on autopilot and suggested several titles that I knew were in the range of his reading level and loosely fit the types of books I knew he liked to read. The truth, though? I had never read those books myself. They were more like the books I knew I should suggest rather than a true book recommendation that came from a thoughtful, informed place.

Of course, Munchkin called me on it the next day: "Those books were no good. They were lame. Try again, Mrs. Scoggin. You love to read. You have to know of a book I would like." I opened my mouth to protest and then shut it. He was right. Instead, I asked Munchkin to give me a week. I visited both my school librarian and the public librarian and gathered several titles that sounded promising, along with one or two of the titles I had suggested to Munchkin originally. I began with the titles that I had recommended to him at first. He was right. I totally got schooled by a second grader. I would have never recommended those titles to him had I read the books first. I turned toward the books recommended by the librarians, giving myself permission to abandon those books that didn't hold my interest. After all, if I was going to recommend books, I had to stand by my choices authentically. Obviously, kids can smell a phony and aren't afraid to call us on it. I got some weird looks on the commuter train as I dug into books that were clearly written for children, but I have never been one who is afraid to fly my teacher flag in public. By the end of the week, I had discovered several amazing new books, and as I recommended them to my little friend, it felt so good to truly stand firm in my suggestions. I had read the books, I actually loved the books, and I was confident in how I matched these titles to my reader.

Long story short, spending time actually reading some of the titles that my students read and love has made me a better teacher. Plus, I have discovered titles I truly love that help me connect to my students on a different level. They are pumped that I have read the books, too, and they come running into the classroom ready to share their latest observation with me. Some of them have even come in with suggestions for *my* reading, which is very special. Clearly, it isn't reasonable to expect that you read *every* book in your classroom library, nor is it reasonable to expect an adult to exclusively read children's literature. But we are teachers even when we aren't in our classrooms, and it is reasonable to think about adding children's literature into our own reading rotation. It's better than you remember. For me, the challenge to make the perfect recommendations to my students has pushed me to read books outside my own typical regimen as well as to search harder for new characters, authors, and titles. It is more like an exciting treasure hunt, and when you engage in these types of searches and conversations with your students, connecting to them as readers and validating their reading passion becomes fun and less like another item on your to-do list.

Whole-Group Experiences: The Minilesson

I think if I hear someone talk about "the architecture of the minilesson" one more time, I might throw something. One reason discussions about "the minilesson" make me crazy is that they push this type of instruction into a pretty little box that allows for no flexibility. Before you know it, "the almighty minilesson that must be delivered in this one particular way" becomes your own Sisyphean task. As in, you keep coming back for more when it just isn't working. Instead, let's approach this from a new, slightly less prescriptive angle and have a chat about the purposes and possibilities of the minilesson.

Whole-group lessons, such as the minilesson, give us a chance to model sound reading strategies and expose students to the hows of reading (Allyn, 2007, 2012; Diller, 2007). This is when we expose all of our friends to grade-level material, strategies, and expectations. In breaking a minilesson down, there are a few key things you need to consider doing to make your teaching tight and relevant. Regardless of the terminology, you want to do the following: Connect your current teaching back to your previous teaching, teach one idea explicitly through clear modeling and thinking aloud, allow students an opportunity to quickly practice what it is you would like them to do, and then send them off by reiterating your key teaching point and their work for the day. These components are typically presented in that order, but there are moments when you need to change things up to keep your teaching fresh or to better fit the needs of your instruction. Whatever you need to do to keep your instruction clear, engaging, and joyful, do that. I mean, I'm not advocating that you go totally rogue and start delivering 45-minute lectures to your fourth graders while standing atop a desk, but I think you get what I am saying. The literacy block should not be about rigidity; it should be about flexibility to meet students' needs and your own while holding true to the principles of good instruction.

Make Connections. When we begin our teaching by connecting to our previous instruction, we accomplish a number of important goals. First, we review key ideas for our students in a brief and clear fashion. Second, we reinforce the idea that our teaching is connected, hopefully allowing our students to see how our work goes together. The goal is to make our teaching consistently deepen and build as the year continues; sometimes thinking through how the discrete teaching point of one day connects to our previous work allows us to see the forest for the trees as well. Teachers are busy people, and it is easy to get bogged down in checking the box of teaching a particular skill when the powerful choice is to work with our students to build a repertoire or reading practice and strategies.

The key here is to keep your teaching brief and to the point. This is merely the introduction to your main teaching for the day. If you feel the need to do a full-blown 20-minute review of past instruction, perhaps you should make the review itself your focus of the day rather than moving on to introduce another key idea after asking students to listen intently for an extended period of time.

Teach One Idea Explicitly. Pam Allyn (2007, 2012) beautifully highlights the importance of keeping our teaching focused on one single objective. This is much harder than it sounds. Often, when our teaching begins to feel lengthy or overly complicated, it is because we are trying to teach too many ideas at the same time. This holy-cow-my-lesson-is-feeling-muddled-even-to-me feeling is a signal that we need to pause, reflect, and pare back what we were trying to accomplish with that particular lesson. When we ask students to focus on a single objective, our teaching retains a level of clarity that allows students to truly focus on and walk away with an idea of what they should be working on as readers.

Most of the thoughts that really good readers have as they read happen quietly inside their minds. Therefore, it is our responsibility to make this sort of thinking evident and clear to students as we model what we would like them to try as readers. By thinking aloud as we engage with a text, we can make the thought processes the focus of our teaching, rather than one individual piece of text. You might say, "Listen as I think about…." You may also want to review your thought processes at the close of your lesson: "Did you hear how I first noticed what my character was saying, then I thought about what that teaches me about that character, and last I chose a word or two to add to my description of that character?" Clearly modeling our thinking for our students allows them to hear examples of the work good readers do as they engage with a text.

Allow Students a Chance to Try. Of course, we want students to give our teaching objectives a try as they work with texts of their choice. However, in the spirit of gradually releasing the responsibility back to students, it is ideal to give them the opportunity to try this new idea right there with you in your teaching area. This work may take the form of students turning and talking to one another, students stopping to jot an idea on a scrap of paper, students thinking independently about an idea to share, or a larger group conversation. The goal is to allow them to briefly try out this new idea or strategy with a familiar text, and to give you a chance to gauge their level of understanding. This is a key moment to observe the work of your students so you can adjust your instruction accordingly. For example, I recently taught a lesson during which I asked second graders to use the look of the font, the information from the picture, and what was happening in the story to help decide how to use their voices as readers. When I asked students to take a closer look at one particular page from a familiar read-aloud and discuss with a partner how they might use their voices as they read that section and why, I noticed that students were only referring to the font and the illustration. By making my way around the rug and listening in on student conversations, I knew that it would be essential for me to highlight how to use the content of the story itself to direct the tone of my reading in my upcoming read-aloud.

Send Students Away With Something to Do. At this point in your lesson, you have connected your teaching to the larger body of your instruction, beautifully taught students one new idea to try as readers, and given them a moment to try out this new idea as you listen in to adjust future instruction. Our work is a thing of teaching beauty. In the home stretch, it is important to think through a clear and brief sentence or two that refocuses children exactly on their work for the day and what you would like them to try as readers. You may want to take a moment to add this new idea to an anchor chart or other classroom artifact. Referents such as these allow students to be more independent and to easily recall key information without relying exclusively on you to be the expert in the room.

So, we know that the minilesson is intended to deliver grade-level instruction in logical, appropriate steps that fit the general needs of your class, but let's talk turkey for a moment, shall we? Not all of your little lovelies are reading on grade level, are they? What else is new, right? That's why it is key to keep this whole-group direct instructional time tight and explicit. No more going on and on about how to infer what a character might be thinking. No more example after example, because all of these examples, although I am sure they are fantastic, take time away from students being able to read and practice these new ideas in their own reading. In short, less talking means more reading.

Minilessons can very quickly become maxilessons when too much teacher talk gets involved. I can admit that I love to talk, and sometimes it feels like the more we talk and the more we model and the more examples we give, the more likely it is that our little friends will get what we are talking about. Maybe. However, it is more likely that our little friends will tune out or learn to dislike the literacy block because "that woman just won't stop talking." Let me give you a few tips for keeping your instruction focused and tight that are based on watching many teachers talk for a long time.

First, when you connect your work for the day back to prior teaching, that doesn't mean launching into an extensive review of an entire unit's worth of teaching. It means a quick statement or two that orients students' thinking and prepares them for what you are about to say today. Second, don't wing your modeling. If you are using a text, mark the page(s) you want to use. If you are going to think aloud, plan your think-alouds in advance, taking care to space them out purposefully. In a minilesson, you typically model one time what you would like students to do, so make it clear and purposeful. Third, never read an entire book aloud during a minilesson. That is a surefire way to make your minilesson muddled and very long. If you know that you would like to refer to a specific section of a text during a particular minilesson, make sure that you read that section in advance of teaching that lesson. Do it as a read-aloud the day before. That way, you are only referring to familiar texts with children during your minilesson and can quickly and more effectively zero in on what it is you would like students to notice you doing and thinking. This means careful, strategic planning and looking at what you might do over the course of an entire week, rather than a day at a time. Finally, carefully craft the opportunity for your students to try what it is you would like them to do as readers. Do they need to bring anything to your meeting area? Make sure they do that in advance, not during the lesson, which is distracting and a time eater. Do you want them to turn and talk, stop and jot, or find something in their own reading? We are talking about 10–15 minutes of instructional time. I can't tell you to spend three hours planning 15 minutes of your day, but I can tell you that spending 20–30 minutes thinking through and envisioning the turns in your teaching in advance of actually doing a lesson will make for a better presentation to your students, and it is work that will endure and save you time year after year. How can that not make you smile?

Whole-Group Experiences: The Read-Aloud

When I would fantasize about being a teacher (yes, I fantasized about being a teacher when I was younger), I would also imagine myself reading aloud to a rapt group of children. I have a flair for the dramatic, so clearly kids who were captivated and sharing texts was an integral part of what I thought it meant to be a teacher. I loved it when my teacher read aloud to the class. I love sharing books with other people. Although I now need to add the element of strategic and purposeful instruction to my read-alouds, I never want to lose that sense of joy for myself or for my students. Reading aloud and sharing books together is fun. It should stay fun. Incorporating a discussion about the theme, a character change, or the importance of the setting should never feel intrusive or like a Debbie Downer. Rather, these conversations should feel organic to students and part of the exciting banter that comes along with sharing a text. Keeping our read-alouds light is up to us; it's all in the delivery.

Read-alouds are another whole-group guided experience in which we can model and practice various skills and strategies with and alongside our students. Another key purpose of the read-aloud is to expose children to a wide variety of authors, genres, text types, and subjects. Read-aloud time should be highly anticipated, sacred, and routine in your classroom. Read-alouds are not something to wing in the spur of the moment. This does not mean that I am not a fan of the teachable moment. However, the teachable moment only arises when we choose to go down a different path from what we originally planned because of the needs of our class in that very moment. When you follow the lead of your students in the absence of a plan and land on something fabulous, that is called luck, not a teachable moment. I think you see where I am going here: The key to including purposeful, instructionally appropriate read-alouds in your day in joyful ways takes thoughtful planning.

One of the biggest reasons I love read-alouds, besides the opportunity to let my dramatic side shine through (you should hear the voices I do in a heated round of *Strega Nona* by Tomie dePaola!) is that they provide your struggling readers with the chance to flex their reading muscles with more complex texts. Many times, I found that my students who had trouble unlocking their reading independently were able to contribute moments of brilliance to our discussion when I took responsibility for the reading. It is essential that we give our students this opportunity and let them surprise us with what they can do, rather than continuing to focus on their areas of challenge. You know how it feels when the student you least expect raises a hand and says something that blows you away. This is when that can happen.

Prior to sharing any given read-aloud with your class, take time to think through a few questions. First, does your read-aloud need to be split into chunks across a number of days to allow for ample time for your students to process and engage with the text? If so, where are the logical stopping points that help facilitate your conversation while providing clear opportunities for you to model or for students to practice the desired skill or strategy? Second, can you make any other connections to the read-aloud from other areas of your day, such as social studies or science? (Remember when we had time for those?) Connecting our reading across the day helps students to see the purpose of reading in a variety of areas and gets you a bit more bang for your buck. Now, as you dig into your read-aloud, think carefully about where you will stop to think aloud, ask a question, or model a particular skill. Do not wing this. I know that we all think we can because we are amazing, but trust me, you will overdo it or underdo it. Select the best moments to stop, and mark those with sticky notes. Script your question for yourself. Envision your think-aloud: What will you say?

Amid all of this planning and strategy forming, never forget the power of your delivery. Although we may be working to make sure students get another opportunity to try a challenging skill or strategy, we never want to let our read-alouds stray into, well, sucking. Imagine me at your side telling you to edit, edit, edit. Edit your turns and talks, your moments to think aloud, and your questions to ensure that the joy of the story itself doesn't get overshadowed. I think Kelly Gallagher (2009) is a wise man when he writes that too many teachers kill students' love of reading by asking them to stop and jot, turn and talk, or stop and think so many times that they can no longer fall in love with the story itself. Think about the last book you read: How many times did you stop to jot something on a sticky note, or have someone interrupt your flow with a thought-provoking question? I'm guessing that you just enjoyed your coffee and some quiet time with a book. Although we are responsible for pushing students' ability to take apart and consume texts, we are also responsible for fostering a love of reading, not an addiction to sticky notes.

Some of you are reading this right now and thinking, This woman thinks I have all the time in the world to plan a read-aloud! What about the laundry or math? Granted, I tend to short things like my math because of calculators and, frankly, because I think reading is more fun. But I am not talking about taking 60 minutes to plan a 20-minute read-aloud; that does not yield a good return on your investment. (See? Math talk. I can do it.) Flipping through a chapter or a picture book for 5–10 minutes and making thoughtful decisions about your teaching moves is doable. It's reasonable. And if you use super sticky notes, your planning will endure, meaning you can take advantage of your own time investment for years to come.

Small-Group Experiences: The Small Group

The purpose of small-group instruction is to meet the needs of all the students in your classroom regardless of their reading level (Allyn, 2007, 2012; Diller, 2007). This is when you deliver instruction that is specifically catered to a particular student or group of students. It is powerful stuff mainly because you control the group of students, the text being used, and the teaching point being addressed, taking care to ensure that all of these stars align to create instructional magic. During small-group instruction, you scaffold students' learning so they slowly take greater and greater responsibility and, ultimately, make sure they do more of the work than you. Also known as a gradual release of responsibility (Fisher, Frey, & Lapp, 2011), this idea prioritizes the idea of student independence. Of course, doing this well assumes that you know your students well, are aware of what they can do successfully and independently, and purposefully build on this base one step at a time.

It is essential that your small groups be flexible. Students are rearranged into groups throughout the year as their needs shift and patterns within your class change. Effective small-group work isn't about assigning students to a status (frequently referred to as the "highs," "mediums," and "lows"); it's about finding groups of students with similar needs. Students clustered around a particular need can be from a range of independent reading levels. You can choose to have your groups shift organically as your teacher's intuition tells you it's time to shake things up. Or, you can choose the more methodical route and stick a brightly colored sticky note in your planner every six to eight weeks as a reminder to rethink the groups you currently have going.

I can almost hear you thinking, Well, how many times a week am I supposed to meet with each of these groups? I can't possibly meet with all of my groups every day. No, you can't meet with every group every day. That is crazy talk. As Debbie Diller (2007) states, "It's not about how many groups you can 'fit into' a day. Rather, it's about meeting the needs of students in small groups" (p. 31). Ease into the waters. Lay out a plan so you are meeting with each group in a configuration that meets the needs of your instruction. Remember, equity doesn't always mean equality. Maybe you want me to give you a recipe right now—an equation that tells you to meet with this type of group three times and this other type of group two times. I am not going to do that. It might feel good for a while to think you have found the "right" way to do it, but the truth is that the right way to do it is more flexible than that. For example, do you need to meet with a group struggling with fluency every day for four days before releasing them to do some extensive practice with repeated readings of familiar texts? Do you need to meet with another group working on accumulating key events across longer chunks of text once every three days so they have time in between your meetings to read extensively? This means you may need to revisit your schedule every time your groups change, creating a new schedule that suits the needs of your instruction and gives students ample time to practice their way toward independence.

Small-Group Experiences: The Conference

Conferring Is More Than Just Having a Chat. Almost every teacher I have ever met loves the idea of sitting one on one with a child to discuss his or her reading. We all know that it is a time to truly tailor our instruction, delivering precisely what one student needs in that moment while getting in some serious bonding time to boot. However, if you happen to mention the logistics of conferring with readers to some teachers, you may just have yourself a front row seat for some serious complaining. It will begin with the frustration of how one might take and organize decent conferring notes and end with—well, it might never end. I hear you. Conferring can be a challenge, from finding time, to feeling like you are meeting with everyone equitably, to "Where the heck is my clipboard?" However, before chalking conferring up to one of those it-would-be-nice practices that never seem to fit in an actual classroom without driving you bananas, let's break it down.

One purpose of holding reading conferences is to hear your students read and to have an opportunity to talk with them one on one about their reading lives. Another purpose of strong conferring work is to meet the individual needs of students through focused one-on-one instruction.

Finally, conferring allows us to get to know our students better as readers and help shape or expand their preferences and habits. When we break conferring work down into those three fairly clear-cut purposes, it sounds lovely, doesn't it? When done well and without all the stress related to time and equity, conferring work can and should become central to your practice for many reasons. First of all, it is beneficial for your students to receive this sort of individualized attention. Beyond that, conferring with your readers allows you as a reading teacher to form strong connections to your students, a goal repeatedly cited as key for teacher happiness. I don't know about you, but being able to sit and connect to my little friends about their reading lives not only makes me feel like I have accomplished something important but also almost always brings a smile to my face.

The Ins and Outs of a Successful Reading Conference. So, let's talk through a few aspects of conferring with readers that teachers frequently find to be a source of stress and work to turn that frown upside down. One frustration that I hear repeated many times over is not knowing what to do with a student once you find yourself sitting next to him or her. Wouldn't it be nice if you could just snuggle up to a little friend, listen to him or her read, or chat together for a few minutes, and bam! Just like that, out of the heavens, genius would strike you with an amazing, spectacular, awe-inspiring teaching point! Divine teacher intervention! Although that would be fantastic, it is unlikely. I love a teachable moment as much as the next girl, but going with a teachable moment doesn't mean never having a plan. Instead, I suggest looking to three sources when considering what you might wish to accomplish with any given student during your reading conferences. The first is any data you gather while administering a useful formal assessment, such as a running record. The second is your knowledge of the instructional level of the student: What are the particular features of that level? What do children have to be able to do as readers to be successful with that particular level of text? Finally, turn to your own observations and anecdotal notes: How does that student engage with your whole-group lessons? What have you observed about the student's reading habits?

At the beginning of the year, my reading conferences are exploratory in nature. I want to get to know the readers, their preferences, their habits, and their past experiences with and attitudes toward reading. I am an avid kid watcher; I notice who raises a hand, who relies on a partner too heavily, who pretends to read, and who never takes a book home. Once we are a few weeks in and our culture of readers is beginning to gel, I turn to an assessment such as a running record to give me more specific information. As I administer my running record, I keep an index card handy with that student's name written across the top and jot down struggles and strengths as they occur to me. I find that some of my best thoughts are running through my brain in that moment and can't be re-created at home. Hence, I jot them down in the moment rather than setting myself up for a very unhappy evening of desperately trying to recall how it all went down. I then take those notes and look for patterns. I try to determine which hurdle I would like to tackle first with each student and then come up with a plan of what I would like to accomplish in each conference for the next few meetings. I transfer this goal and my rough plan to the note-taking sheet I use for my conferences. I really need this type of reminder in my face while sitting with a student; I mean, the interruptions of random announcements alone are enough to throw any girl off her game.

Does that sound like a lot? It really isn't. My original notes are taken during the administration of the running record and therefore do not take any additional time at home or after school. Looking through my notes and putting a plan in place can be time-consuming, maybe 15 minutes per student on average. But think about it: That initial investment of time sets me up to hold productive, focused conferences for the next six weeks or so. To me, that seems like a good return on my investment. Plus, feeling that confident about my work with students is priceless.

OK, I can hear you wondering about the logistics of scheduling reading conferences from here. First of all, can I suggest that you actually go over to the student rather than calling the student back to your table of intimidation? Let's not waste any minutes when students can be reading by adding yet another transition into the day. Plus, as we move throughout the room to have these conversations with our students, we spread our influence around and can mitigate several potential behavioral issues. I also find that while I am talking to one student, I have two or three others lurking. They think they are sly, but I can see them listening, and I welcome the eavesdropping! We could definitely have bigger problems than that!

I am going to try to break this to you gently: There is no magic formula of reading conference perfection. I wish there were, but just like everything else in education, the silver bullet eludes us because of the various nuances in each and every classroom. (OK, I don't *really* wish there was a one-size-fits-all answer, but I get how it would make life easier if I could say, "Three conferences a day will make all of your students avid, successful readers.") The reality is that planning and scheduling your reading conferences is a bit of a logic puzzle. What I can do is give you some of my hard-earned advice to consider so the schedule you create is in line with best practices and doesn't give you crazy face. First of all, let's talk time. How much time do you *really* have to confer with students? Not how much time do you feel like you should have or how much time does someone else say you should have, but how much time do you really have when you lay your instructional cards on the table? Now that you have a realistic time frame in mind, put scheduling and time to the side. Yes, you heard me correctly. We are going to put time and how many conferences you think you can get to and how long you believe the perfect conference is aside. The reality is that there is no perfect schedule, no magic formula of how many kids you should meet with in a given day, and no magic number of minutes that a conference should last. I have watched one too many teachers (myself included) drive themselves crazy over trying to fit the needs of the students into a predetermined schedule that just doesn't work. So, let's stop putting time or the schedule at the center of our planning and instead shift to place our students' needs at the center of our planning.

I can hear you gasping from here.

Now you have a choice to make. You can schedule your students to have a routine conference with you every so many days. In this scenario, your schedule is relatively set; yes, you can change it up in a few weeks, but in general, the same kids meet with you on day 1, day 2, day 3, and so on. This ensures that you can get to every student at least one time in a one-on-one format every two or three weeks. For some of you, this works beautifully. But for the rest of us, who find ourselves continuously banging our heads against the wall trying to make a schedule work, let's allow our students' needs to drive the bus, not the clock. Create a more flexible schedule that is determined by the needs of the students by considering the first goal that you would like to tackle with each of your students as readers. Are there any patterns that emerge or groups of children who can meet with you together? Do some students have very specific goals that are not similar to those of their peers, and need intensive conferring work? What format, a conference or a small group, will best allow you to teach into that particular goal?

Once you have considered these questions, take a look at the actual time you have to work with your readers over the next four to six weeks or so. How can you fit in the right combination of small-group work and conferences to meet the needs of your students? For example, you might have a few students who need to focus on book choice and therefore would benefit from a conference every day for two or three days while they create a reading plan. These same students might then need a week without a conference to allow them to fall into their reading. Other students might need to check in every other day so you can see if they are adequately accumulating the text. Still other students may only need a conference every six or seven days to push their thinking once they have completed several books. In this second choice, you still need to consider the amount of time you actually have each day to confer, but your scheduled meetings will flex as students' goals and needs flex. I honestly do not think you can go wrong with either decision as long as your decision is thoughtful and purposeful and fits your teaching style. These are the keys to making sound decisions that you can smile about. Regardless of your decision, take care to make sure that students who receive any sort of intervention receive ample time to read alone, without an adult. We want to avoid inadvertently teaching students to be unable to read without someone to hold their hand.

Keeping It All Straight: Organizing Your Conference Notes. As many of you may already know, I consider myself a bit of an organizational goddess. I heart the organizing. I welcome a good trip to Staples. I am that person in the home office section of Target exclaiming loudly about the new chevron-striped clipboards. I almost had a stroke when Sharpie came out with fine-point felt-tipped pens that don't bleed through the paper. I mean, how do they do that?! I have also witnessed a number of excellent teachers go down in flames because they couldn't just pick a system for organizing reading conference notes. Let's just get a little reality out of the way and admit that no system is perfect and that at a certain point, you just have to pick one and go with it. Let's also be real with ourselves and admit how much happier we can make ourselves feel during the day by purchasing a cool new app, a cute clipboard, or a new pack of our favorite pens. So, step 1 to feeling more Zen about your conference notes is to buy stuff that makes you smile; you're already spending a lot of your own money on other classroom supplies, so you might as well splurge a bit on yourself.

I can be a bit old-school when it comes to keeping and organizing conference notes. I like a clipboard with one note-taking sheet for every child in my class. Each sheet has several spaces so I can record information from five or six conferences or small groups in one place to track my work over time. My conferring sheet also has a space for goals at the top; I make sure to write my goal for that student as a reader clearly at the top of each page. I am not that old, but I do have two children, and they have not improved my memory. Combine that with the constant interruptions that seem to punctuate the school day, and you have a recipe for never getting anything done unless you write it down. I also have a stack of sticky notes or index cards in a baggy clipped in with my conference sheets. I never have to stray far to get what I need, which means I (almost) never have to break the all-mighty reading conference magic to jump up and grab a sticky note. Once I fill up my conferring sheets, I save them in an equally chic binder with a separate section for each student. I am not doing the rain forest any favors with my paper-bound system, but it works for me, and if I can raise a reader who ultimately saves the rain forests, I feel like the two even out.

My super colleagues have a range of methods for taking conference notes that are equally amazing. Some use sticky notes or peel-and-stick labels that are then transferred to a master sheet or notebook page reserved for that particular student. Others have a notebook that they have sectioned off with a set of pages for each student. Still others have created conference sheets that they leave behind with students as a reminder of the discussions and goals that have been set.

Are you ready to get fancy? Let's chat for a moment about taking conference notes on your tablet. I have dipped my toes into these technological waters because I think it will ultimately yield more comprehensive notes that I will be able to reference both at home and at school and because I feel as if it is key to model for students purposeful ways to integrate technology into our lives. I know several teachers who are using the app Confer that was specially designed to help teachers create groups, record notes, and organize students. It's pretty hot from what I hear, but I am totally digging Evernote for conferring. One of my super colleagues suggested it to me. Get this: Using Evernote on your smartphone to take conference notes allows you to take photographs of student work, the artifact you left behind, or what students are reading and include that in your notes. You can also record your conversation or a snippet of a student reading aloud and upload it to your notes. Using creative tags, you can organize your notes by student and by skill for easy sorting. Last but not least, you can share your notebook of conference notes with an administrator or colleague to help facilitate collaboration.

The bottom line is that there are a million ways to take and organize your conference notes, so you can find a system that fits your personal style and comfort level. The key here is that you are taking reliable and useful conference notes that help shape your future instruction. If you are simply filling out a box with a bunch of information that leaves you at a loss for what to do with that student the next time you meet, you are writing down the wrong stuff. So, stop, take a breath, and consider what you could write down that would be helpful as you move forward with that student. For me, it took years of writing down the title of what that student was reading to realize that I almost never referenced this information when thinking through my instruction. Instead, it was key for me to jot down the moves in my own teaching (and the student's response to those moves) to ensure that I could thoughtfully and gradually release the responsibility back to the student to promote independence.

> Teaching matters, but what kind of teaching matters most? Where is the reading sweet spot? It certainly is not found buried in a 122-page curriculum guide. However, it is also not found when we hand students books that are too difficult for them and ask them to navigate on their own. The sweet spot lies somewhere between these two extreme instructional approaches. (Gallagher, 2009, p. 90)

It's All About Balance

There are two ways you can digest this chapter: The first is to have a total panic attack and then commit yourself to a rigid and overly optimistic schedule that leaves you feeling as if you are failing on a daily basis. An unrealistic, inflexible schedule can be just as limiting as a curriculum guide that prescribes every move you make. I know you want to see all of your kids in a conference in the course of one week. I know you want to meet with all of your groups at least three times a week. I know you beat yourself up about not doing enough at all times. I know.

Take a deep breath and realize that this feeling of constantly letting your students down despite teaching to the limits of your very soul is not the sweet spot that Gallagher (2009) is referring to. It is painful for you and bound to be reflected in your instruction despite your best efforts.

The second way you could digest this chapter is to realize that the key to balancing these moving parts is to make thoughtful and purposeful decisions that are tied to the needs of your students. Creating a schedule and maintaining your teaching stamina depend on your ability to make wise choices and invest time and energy in planning. An up-front investment of planning time releases you to spend the next six to eight weeks focused on your teaching and relishing a connection to your students as readers. Think about it: You can invest time each and every evening thinking about what you are going to do tomorrow, and then stress before you meet with each student, your mind racing to come up with a teaching point, or you can spend a few hours gathering your thoughts over a latte and then do quick maintenance each evening to just refresh yourself on your course of action. I don't want to be pushy or anything, but I think the choice is pretty obvious: Always choose the option that involves sipping a latte.

> Trying to see every group every day will not yield quality teaching. Remember, *quality, not quantity*. It's not about how many groups you can "fit into" a day. Rather, it's about meeting the needs of students in small groups. (Diller, 2007, p. 31)

As you move forward with your own planning and attempt to solve the logic puzzle that is scheduling your reading block of instruction, be mindful of modeling flexible thinking and action for your students. That's what we want for them, right—to be flexible thinkers and doers when confronted with a complex problem? With this focus on flexibility comes the permission to meet with small groups and individual students in ways that best meet both the needs of the students and your needs as a teacher. One week it might mean several intensive small groups followed by another week of conferences aimed at maintenance and individualization. Then, rinse and repeat. As you move forward and see progress, you may wish to change things up, allowing more time for conferences and using small groups intermittently to solidify and share student learning. Each plan is thoughtful, purposeful, and shaped by the needs of your students. Each plan is realistic and possible to accomplish within the actual time that you have dedicated to reading instruction. Each plan allows you and your students space to breathe, to block out the noise of outside media and its panic mentality, and to feel the joy that is reading.

CHAPTER 7

Let's Get Fabulous

Why We Need to Take Back Control Over Our Teaching

> *It takes courage to stand up to absurdity when all around you people remain comfortably seated. But if we need one more reason to do the right thing, consider this: The kids are watching us, deciding how to live their lives in part by how we've chosen to live ours.*
>
> —Alfie Kohn (2013, para. 17)

During my doctoral work, I was fortunate enough to take a course in social imagination with Maxine Greene, which is such a nerdy reference that I may have already lost many of you. Let me just say this: Maxine Greene was badass. She may have been in her 90s, but she could reference classic educational theory, the latest presidential address, and a *Vanity Fair* article in the same breath. On top of all of that, she was a genius about what it means to educate children. I spent every week sitting in her living room (which we called "the salon"—I mean, nerd fest!), letting her stories, passion, and optimistic view of possibility in education wash over me like academic medicine. One afternoon, she said that the ridiculousness of education all boils down to the fact that teachers are expected to cultivate a sense of curiosity, encourage creative problem solving, and instill a love of learning in children when they themselves are not expected or allowed to behave in similar ways. Schools are slowly becoming places of impossibility, rather than places of possibility for both teachers and children. It was all I could do not to leap from the couch, shout, "Yes! You nailed it!" and high-five Maxine.

Let Your Reading Life Be Your Guide

So, if we want to bestow upon our little friends a love of learning and a passion for reading, we have to find our own spaces to live an active reading life as well. We also have to find ways to let this active reading life bleed over into our professional life in ways that not only push our practice but also leave us feeling happy and professionally fulfilled. No one needs an extra to-do item on their plate that doesn't lead in these directions. Some might call me a me-monster because I frequently toot my own horn, but reflecting on my own life as a reader has been immensely effective in my teaching of reading. However, as a teacher of reading, I have often found that reflecting on my own reading life and processes is immensely helpful when considering my future instructional moves. So, yes, I am advocating for more me-monster time, but before you write me off completely, allow me to share what I have realized about myself and how that impacts my own reading instruction.

> Without question, I am a better teacher because I read. I pass books into my students' hands and talk with them about what they read. I model what a reading life looks like and show my students how reading enriches my life and can enrich theirs, too. (Miller, 2014, p. 6)

Perhaps most important is that I know that simply the fact that I have a reading life is a step toward becoming a more effective teacher of reading.

Kids can smell a phony a mile away. If you approach a group of children and claim, "This is one of my favorite books," in that weird singsongy teacher voice when really you think that particular book is the pits, they will be onto you in a second. We can't claim to be something we aren't, nor can we ask our students to engage in ways that we are unwilling to engage in ourselves. If you have never thought about your reading life before, get started. If you don't feel as if you have time to read, I get it. I could easily spend every spare moment of my life doing laundry. How two small people create so much laundry is beyond me; I spend so much time in that little laundry room that I have considered putting in a wet bar to just spice things up a bit. But I digress. What I am trying to say is that I hear you. We are all busy. But if we want to claim to students that the act of reading is so essential, it needs to be essential to our own lives. Put the laundry basket down and take 10 minutes to read a book. The laundry will still be there. Believe me.

When I think about myself as a reader, I know that I read a *wide* range of texts. I always have a downloaded book on my phone, and I read a number of blogs daily through a blog reader app. I click on articles that my friends link to Facebook, watch videos, and view photographs. If you take a snapshot of my nightstand, you will probably see an academic journal with a pen jammed in as a bookmark, some sort of book about teaching or reading, a stack of fiction from my mother or the library, *Baby 411: Clear Answers and Smart Advice for Your Baby's First Year*, and three weeks' worth of *People, Cooking Light,* and *HGTV* magazines. My husband loves to pass me off as his super smart wife who is single-handedly teaching the world to read, one child at a time. Then, one of his colleagues saw me reading a *People* magazine and almost tripped over his own shock. "*You* read *People* magazine?!" he said aghast. "Um, yes, obsessively. But only the really vapid parts about celebrities. Oh, and the book reviews," I said. "But I thought you had your doctorate!" he cried. "I do. This is how I survived." The lesson here? I read texts that are easy and entertaining, I read texts that challenge my thinking and push me to read more slowly, I devour stories, and I enjoy looking at pictures of well-decorated houses. Therefore, as a teacher of reading, I should not always push my students to read classic pieces of literature to the exclusion of other texts. As we push to broaden our own definition of what counts as reading to include videos, photographs, and other highly visual media, we must also allow our students to consume these forms of text, validating and celebrating them. Just like I need my *People* magazine fix, our students should be allowed to embrace a range of texts—some that are too easy, some that are very challenging, some that push them to think deeply, and some that allow their minds to take a break.

Here is another one of my reading secrets: I skim. (I think I heard you gasp from here.) Yes, I skim—often. Did I not just mention the amount of laundry I have? There is no way I would be able to make my way through the stack on my nightstand if I didn't occasionally skim my way through reading. I skim *People* magazine to find pieces about famous people I still recognize, and I skim books about the teaching of reading to find sections related to my specific need or interest. So, when I look to the reading habits of my students, it becomes a bit hypocritical to ask them to read each and every text they encounter deeply and multiple times. Sometimes you just need to skim and move on. It is all about balance.

I spent years feeling guilty about abandoning Amy Tan's *The Joy Luck Club.* I just could not get into that book and ended up putting it aside. Prior to this, I had never left a book unfinished, no matter how painful. We can't love every book we pick up, and therefore, we can't force our students to stick with every book they pick up. That book with the jaunty cover that some small fry picked up because it looked cool and in reality is totally lame? Put it back. Don't make that student suffer. Now, when you have someone who chronically abandons books, that's another issue. But coming across a dud now and then? It happens. Move on.

Finally, when I think about myself as a reader, I realize that I am never without something to read, but sometimes I am not sure what text to turn to next. I read in waves. There are stretches of weeks when I devour books like they are made of bacon. These times are unpredictable; my last stretch of rabid reading came out of left field while I was up at all hours of the night with my newborn son. Who knew that sleep deprivation and endless hours of rocking a baby would equal a reading binge? I found that downloading books to my phone and reading them while walking lap after lap around his nursery made the hours feel less insane and evened out my level of frustration. There were actually times when he would cry at 4 a.m. and I would think, Well, at least I get to read the next chapter of *Gone Girl.* Maybe it's something that only a truly sleep-deprived parent can understand, but I think you get what I am saying. Right now, I am obsessively reading short blog posts and magazine articles but am unsure of what book to turn to next—young adult or a book purely for myself? Over these periods of indecision, I developed coping strategies that allow me to keep reading while thinking about my next move as a reader. This is what real reading looks like, and therefore, I need to teach my students how to develop similar strategies. Students need to have a reading plan, strategies for finding time to read, and ways to keep themselves reading when they feel stuck. We also need to work extensively with students to expand and define their tastes as readers so that when they have exhausted a particular author or genre, they know where to turn next and aren't left without a plan. You will not see these ideas reflected in a list of standards, but they are important and real skills that must be developed to foster students who read often and for pleasure. (P.S. Standards aren't the be-all and end-all; there is so much more to the teaching of reading beyond the standards themselves.)

So, I have all the lessons I have learned about myself as a reader that I would like to bring to my practice. I have a strong philosophical notion of what it means to be an effective teacher of reading that I would like to bring to my practice. I have a solid knowledge of the research on best practices in the teaching of reading that I would like to bring to my practice. What does that look like? How do I get to infuse more of myself into my work in the classroom? Cue the fabulous!

It Is Time to Be Fabulous

People who are not teachers have no idea just how challenging and amazing this job can be. We have tightly smiled and restrained ourselves in front of people who feel free to make jokes and openly share their thoughts about our profession without any sort of filter or discretion: "Teaching coloring must be *so* hard." "It must be nice to have your summers off!" "I would *love* to be done with work at 2:00 every day." "You get to spend the whole day playing with kids. That doesn't sound so hard." "Those who can, do. Those who can't, teach." The reality is that teachers are charged with a massive responsibility yet given very little or no control over their work (Ingersoll, 2007). One hand is holding us up while telling us that we have been chosen to raise the next generation of readers, an awesomely important task. The other hand is patting us on the head while simultaneously telling us that we are unable to figure out how to do that: "Just follow the pages in this manual, and you will be fine."

So many nonteachers tinker around with schools, layering on all sorts of accountability measures to make sure that we don't step out of line, essentially tying our hands when it comes to truly addressing the needs of our students. The same individuals who hold up their "research-based claims" ignore the research that highlights the importance of teacher autonomy, collaboration, and empowerment when seeking effective school change (Powell, 2002). I can practically hear them saying, "Oh, thaaaaat," from here. Yes, that. I want to talk about that. I want to talk about the fact that you cannot bully teachers into a one-size-fits-all box that does nothing but damage our students and our souls.

The thing that makes me feel the most frustrated is that the research on the importance of teacher autonomy and empowerment is not new. As far back as the early 1990s, researchers were proclaiming the importance of teacher involvement and empowerment (Black, 1997; Hargreaves, 1994; Heck & Brandon, 1995; Rice & Schneider, 1994; White, 1992). White states that the more a teacher feels involved and included in key decision making, the more likely the teacher will become reenergized in his or her teaching. That's *key* decision making, as in how to use our time, how to meet the needs of our students, how to organize a coherent block of reading instruction, and how to navigate our way toward cultivating avid readers. So, the question now is, Are we going to continue to wait for someone to provide us with the opportunity to become more involved, or are we going to begin to create opportunities for ourselves within our own practices?

Sadly, I have witnessed too many teachers downplaying their fabulousness. I will never understand this. I am fortunate enough to meet and talk with many teachers from all sorts of schools on a regular basis. I see them do amazing things. When I shout, "Yes! Let's share this! It's amazing!" I am all too often met with a no with one of three distinct reasons. The first is a fear of getting caught by the administration. The second is a fear of being ostracized by colleagues who will think you are creating a situation in which they will all be expected to work this hard. The third is a fear of being perceived as showing off. Are we afraid of thinking outside the box, setting a high standard for our work, and being fabulous?

In this book, we have chatted about ways for you to reclaim your happiness and to be fabulous teachers of reading. My advice is based on my own experiences, research on best practices, and my shameless ability to fly my nerd flag. I am a teacher and a huge nerd. I like new pens. Selecting a new notebook is a bit of an event that I look forward to and take pretty seriously. Organized files make me happy. Planners filled with sticky notes and fresh ideas make me feel successful. Digging into a new book feels equal parts luxurious and exciting. After years of hiding my nerd flag, I now fly it proudly, owning what it means to be me. Let's review a few strategies for reclaiming our fabulousness, shall we?

It all begins with a conscious decision to become happier in your work in the classroom. Teaching reading is intense. It is very easy to go through each day running around and to get stuck waiting for someone else to change the tone of your daily work life. It is time to stop waiting. Make some moves to change your daily routine, in both large and small ways, because happier teachers are more effective teachers. Now that you have put a specific emphasis on your desire to be happier at work, take a moment to reflect on the stories that make up your experience as a teacher. Consider your beliefs about what it means to be an effective teacher of reading. What are your nonnegotiables? What kind of teacher are you not yet?

As you start to change your practice to be more focused on your own happiness, start with making changes to your classroom environment. Deal with your clutter! (Hey, you piles sitting in the corner collecting dust and shameful glances, I am looking at you.) Remember, you don't have to go it alone; involve your students. Transform your classroom into a place that is reflective of what you believe in as well as supportive of your students' independence. Although I know that you are amazing and can work wonders with a stapler, this is not the moment to prioritize your bulletin board prowess. Once you have cleared up all of those piles, turn your energy toward thinking through the data you are required and want to collect over the course of the year, Keep in mind that these two categories of data may yield very different answers. Prioritize the data that actually informs your instruction. Be ruthless: Are you giving out that test because the insight it gives you into your students will be invaluable and you plan to deliver concrete feedback to everyone, or are you giving that test because you always have but don't really look at the results too carefully beyond assigning each student a grade? Like that salad spinner, move these less purposeful or less useful assessments to the back corner of your mental cabinet. They do not merit precious real estate in your mind or on your to-do list.

Take on projects, create lesson plans, and sit on committees because that type of work makes *you* happy and professionally fulfilled, not because you want to outdo another colleague or earn a gold star. If you choose to take on work to receive the praise of others, you are setting yourself up for potential (and likely) disappointment. Why do that? Take pride in your own accomplishments and recognize the accomplishments of others. Align yourself with fellow super colleagues in your building, even if it means searching outside your immediate grade-level team. Model the type of working relationships that you fantasize about at the end of a frustrating week. Take the time to plan thoughtfully and look at the big picture of your instruction beyond the next day or even the next week. Instead of feeling overwhelmed each day by all the components of successful reading instruction, work to let those components (whole-group instruction, one-on-one conferences, small groups, read-alouds, and shared reading) complement one another and balance out your instruction. When these pieces work together, they should allow you to breathe.

Finally, read. Read, read, read. Read books for yourself. Stop feeling guilty when you curl up with a book and a cup of coffee. You should not be getting something else done. You should be practicing what you preach. Read books from your classroom. Read books to help push your thinking as a teacher. Read by yourself. Start a reading group to read with others. Share your reading life with your students and call on the realities of your reading life to help you make decisions about how to guide your students to cultivate a reading life of their own.

> I guess I got my swagger back. (Carter, Anderson, Donn, Carter, & Harrell, 2001, stanza 2)

One day, I was riding the commuter train home from another long day in my classroom, silently fuming about pointless meetings, mountains of data, and colleagues who didn't pull their educational weight. As the train rumbled along, I realized that I had sat in that same seat, silently fuming, every day for the last several weeks. Yet, if someone had asked me if I liked teaching, I would have replied with a resounding, "Yes!" because I actually love teaching. When I think of teaching, I think of my little friends, and I am happy. However, at the end of each day, the kids were the furthest thing from my mind. In that moment, I was so tired of being negative, so sick of being angry, so sad about losing my focus on my students, that I decided to make a change for myself. If becoming a mother has taught me anything, it is that continuing to do the same thing and expecting a different result is insane. (Am I right? At 3 a.m., if rocking to sleep isn't working, you stop rocking. You try something else, anything else, until everyone is asleep and happy.) Why should it be any different in my work life? Why did I expect some magical reform fairy to wave her magic wand and improve morale at my school?

If I left my favorite pen under my pillow, would she swoop down and do away with inside recess, out-of-the-classroom teachers who show up late or not at all, or unproductive meetings?

I knew that I had to change if I wanted my attitude and mood to change. Focusing on your own happiness is not a selfish act. It is a gift for your students (and probably the people with whom you live). A short time later, I found wise words from Pam Allyn (2007) about teaching from a place of gratitude (see the pull quote).

I am grateful to have a job that fills up every corner of my mind and heart. I am grateful that I get to spend time and share my love of reading with some truly amazing little people. I am grateful when a little friend challenges himself or herself with a new book, discovers a new author, or comes to school excited to share stories with me.

What are you grateful for? What about this job and the teaching of reading makes you feel the most inspired? When are you the happiest in your teaching? Be brave. Find the courage to focus on your own happiness.

Be fabulous.

At the end of the day, I return to the questions that guide me: Do I feel complete? Am I complete with what I have done today, what I have done this year? I try to forgive myself for the work I have not yet done, and understand that being complete does not mean being finished or being perfect. It means I have done the best I can.

There is so much to be grateful for. I love the idea of teaching with gratitude, to be able to walk into a classroom and we turn around and say, What am I thankful for today?...

Find your gratitude in your teaching. It is here you will feel most complete. (Allyn, 2007, pp. 186–187)

REFERENCES

Allington, R.L. (2012). *What really matters for struggling readers: Designing research-based programs* (3rd ed.). Boston, MA: Pearson.

Allington, R.L. (2013). What really matters when working with struggling readers. *The Reading Teacher, 66*(7), 520–530. doi:10.1002/TRTR.1154

Allington, R.L., & Cunningham, P.M. (2007). *Schools that work: Where all children read and write* (3rd ed.). Boston, MA: Pearson.

Allyn, P. (2007). *The complete 4 for literacy: How to teach reading and writing through daily lessons, monthly units, and yearlong calendars*. New York, NY: Scholastic.

Allyn, P. (2012). *Be core ready: Powerful, effective steps to implementing and achieving the Common Core State Standards*. Boston, MA: Pearson.

Aronowitz, S., & Giroux, H.A. (1993). *Education: Still under siege* (2nd ed.). Westport, CT: Bergin & Garvey.

Beijaard, D., Meijer, P.C., & Verloop, N. (2004). Reconsidering research on teachers' professional identity. *Teaching and Teacher Education, 20*(2), 107–128.

Black, C. (1997). *Getting out of line: A guide for teachers redefining themselves and their profession*. Thousand Oaks, CA: Corwin.

Blakeney-Williams, M., & Daly, N. (2013). How do teachers use picture books to draw on the cultural and linguistic diversity in their classrooms? *Set, 2013*(2), 44–50.

Britzman, D.P. (1991). *Practice makes practice: A critical study of learning to teach*. Albany, NY: State University of New York Press.

Brown, M., & Ralph, S. (1998). The identification of stress in teachers. In J. Dunham & V. Varma (Eds.), *Stress in teachers: Past, present and future* (pp. 37–56). London, England: Whurr.

Bullough, R.V., Jr. (2011). Hope, happiness, teaching, and learning. In C. Day & J.C.-K. Lee (Eds.), *New understandings of teacher's work: Emotions and educational change* (pp. 15–30). New York, NY: Springer.

Calo, K.M. (2011). Incorporating informational texts in the primary grades: A research-based rationale, practical strategies, and two teachers' experiences. *Early Childhood Education Journal, 39*(4), 291–295. doi:10.1007/s10643-011-0470-0

Carlyle, D., & Woods, P. (2002). *Emotions of teacher stress*. Staffordshire, England: Trentham.

Carter, S., Anderson, D.L., Donn, R., Carter, T.D., & Harrell, R. (2001). All I need [Recorded by Jay-Z]. On *The blueprint* [CD]. New York, NY: Roc-A-Fella.

Cochran-Smith, M., & Lytle, S.L. (1999). The teacher research movement: A decade later. *Educational Researcher, 28*(7), 15–25. doi:10.3102/0013189X028007015

Cohen, R.M. (1995). *Understanding how school change really happens: Reform at Brookville High*. Thousand Oaks, CA: Corwin.

Danielson, C. (2007). The many faces of leadership. *Educational Leadership, 65*(1), 14–19.

Darling-Hammond, L. (1997). *The right to learn: A blueprint for creating schools that work*. San Francisco, CA: Jossey-Bass.

Datnow, A. (2011). Collaboration and contrived collegiality: Revisiting Hargreaves in the age of accountability. *Journal of Educational Change, 12*(2), 147–158. doi:10.1007/s10833-011-9154-1

Dietrich, D., & Ralph, K.S. (1995). Crossing borders: Multicultural literature in the classroom. *The Journal of Educational Issue of Language Minority Students, 15*, 65–75.

Diller, D. (2007). *Making the most of small groups: Differentiation for all.* Portland, ME: Stenhouse.

Dirkswager, E.J. (Ed.). (2002). *Teachers as owners: A key to revitalizing public education.* Lanham, MD: ScarecrowEducation.

Dowd, F.S. (1992). *We're not in Kansas anymore*: Evaluating children's books portraying Native American and Asian cultures. *Childhood Education, 68*(4), 219–224. doi:10.1080/00094056.1992.10520878

Evans, R. (2001). The culture of resistance. In *The Jossey-Bass reader on school reform* (pp. 510–521). San Francisco, CA: Jossey-Bass.

Firestone, W.A., & Pennell, J.R. (1993). Teacher commitment, working conditions, and differential incentive policies. *Review of Educational Research, 63*(4), 489–525.

Fisher, D., Frey, N., & Lapp, D. (2011). Focusing on the participation and engagement gap: A case study on closing the achievement gap. *Journal of Education for Students Placed at Risk, 16*(1), 56–64.

Fountas, I.C., & Pinnell, G.S. (1999). *Matching books to readers: Using leveled books in guided reading, K–3.* Portsmouth, NH: Heinemann.

Freire, P. (1998). *Teachers as cultural workers: Letters to those who dare teach* (D. Macedo, D. Koike, & A. Oliveira, Trans.). Boulder, CO: Westview.

Gallagher, K. (2009). *Readicide: How schools are killing reading and what you can do about it.* Portland, ME: Stenhouse.

Gay, G. (2002). Preparing for culturally responsive teaching. *Journal of Teacher Education, 53*(2), 106–116. doi:10.1177/0022487102053002003

Goodwin, A.L. (1987). Vocational choices and the realities of teaching. In F.S. Bolin & J.M. Falk (Eds.), *Teacher renewal: Professional issues, personal choices* (pp. 30–36). New York, NY: Teachers College Press.

Greene, M. (1998). Introduction: Teaching for social justice. In W. Ayers, J.A. Hunt, & T. Quinn (Eds.), *Teaching for social justice* (pp. xxvii–xlvi). New York, NY: New & Teachers College Press.

Hargreaves, A. (1994). *Changing teachers, changing times: Teachers' work and culture in the postmodern age.* New York, NY: Teachers College Press.

Heck, R.H., & Brandon, P.R. (1995). Teacher empowerment and the implementation of school-based reform. *Empowerment in Organizations, 3*(4), 10–19. doi:10.1108/09684899510100325

Hess, F.M. (1999). *Spinning wheels: The politics of urban school reform.* Washington, DC: Brookings Institution Press.

Hiebert, E.H. (Ed.). (2009). *Reading more, reading better.* New York, NY: Guilford.

Ingersoll, R.M. (2007). Short on power, long on responsibility. *Educational Leadership, 65*(1), 20–25.

Johnson, S.M., & Donaldson, M.L. (2007). Overcoming the obstacles to leadership. *Educational Leadership, 65*(1), 8–13.

Joseph, P.B., & Burnaford, G.E. (Eds.). (1994). *Images of school teachers in twentieth-century America: Paragons, polarities, complexities.* Mahwah, NJ: Erlbaum.

Klassen, R.M., & Chiu, M.M. (2010). Effects on teachers' self-efficacy and job satisfaction: Teacher gender, years of experience, and job stress. *Journal of Educational Psychology, 102*(3), 741–756. doi:10.1037/a0019237

Klassen, R.M., Perry, N.E., & Frenzel, A.C. (2012). Teachers' relatedness with students: An underemphasized component of teachers' basic psychological needs. *Journal of Educational Psychology, 104*(1), 150–165.

Kohn, A. (2013, September 16). *Encouraging educator courage.* Retrieved from www.edweek.org/ew/articles/2013/09/18/04kohn.h33.html?tkn=NOWFEYnJYIyyqBanO2RyrIHGcyo7wUMyCKt2&cmp=clp-edweek

Kozol, J. (2005). *The shame of the nation: The restoration of apartheid schooling in America.* New York, NY: Crown.

Kyriacou, C. (1998). Teacher stress: Past and present. In J. Dunham & V. Varma (Eds.), *Stress in teachers: Past, present and future* (pp. 1–13). London, England: Whurr.

Lasky, S. (2005). A sociocultural approach to understanding teacher identity, agency and professional vulnerability in a context of secondary school reform. *Teaching & Teacher Education, 21*(8), 899–916.

Lieberman, A., & Miller, L. (Eds.). (2008). *Teachers in professional communities: Improving teaching and learning.* New York, NY: Teachers College Press.

Llorens, M.B. (1994). Action research: Are teachers finding their voice? *The Elementary School Journal, 95*(1), 3–10. doi:10.1086/461784

Maloch, B., & Horsey, M. (2013). Living inquiry: Learning from and about informational texts in a second-grade classroom. *The Reading Teacher, 66*(6), 475–485.

McDonald, J.P. (1992). *Teaching: Making sense of an uncertain craft.* New York, NY: Teachers College Press.

Miller, D. (2002). *Reading with meaning: Teaching comprehension in the primary grades.* Portland, ME: Stenhouse.

Miller, D. (2008). *Teaching with intention: Defining beliefs, aligning practice, taking action, K–5.* Portland, ME: Stenhouse.

Miller, D. (2009). *The book whisperer: Awakening the inner reader in every child.* San Francisco, CA: Jossey-Bass.

Miller, D. (with Kelley, S.). (2014). *Reading in the wild: The book whisperer's keys to cultivating lifelong reading habits.* San Francisco, CA: Jossey-Bass.

Neuman, S.B. (1999). Books make a difference: A study of access to literacy. *Reading Research Quarterly, 34*(3), 286–311.

Noddings, N. (1994). An ethic of caring and its implications for instructional arrangements. In L. Stone (Ed.), *The education feminism reader* (pp. 171–183). New York, NY: Routledge. (Reprinted from *American Journal of Education, 96*(2), 215–230, 1988)

Pakarinen, E., Kiuru, N., Lerkkanen, M.-K., Poikkeus, A.-M., Siekkinen, M., & Nurmi, J.-E. (2010). Classroom organization and teacher stress predict learning motivation in kindergarten children. *European Journal of Psychology of Education, 25*(3), 281–300. doi:10.1007/s10212-010-0025-6

Parent, M. (2013, February 13). My stories [Web log post]. Retrieved from scarsandstitches.wordpress.com/tag/michael-parent

Payne, C.M. (1998). *So much reform, so little change: Building-level obstacles to urban school reform.* Chicago, IL: Institute for Policy Research, Northwestern University.

Pinar, W.F. (1998). Introduction. In W.F. Pinar (Ed.), *The passionate mind of Maxine Greene: 'I am...not yet.'* Bristol, PA: Falmer.

Powell, L. (2002). Shedding a tier: Flattening organisational structures and employee empowerment. *International Journal of Educational Management, 16*(1), 54–59. doi:10.1108/09513540210415541

Rasinski, T.V., & Padak, N.D. (1990). Multicultural learning through children's literature. *Language Arts, 67*(6), 576–580.

Ravitch, D. (2010). *The death and life of the great American school system: How testing and choice are undermining education* (Rev. ed.). New York, NY: Basic.

Rice, E.M., & Schneider, G.T. (1994). A decade of teacher empowerment: An empirical analysis of teacher involvement in decision making, 1980–1991. *Journal of Educational Administration, 32*(1), 43–58. doi:10.1108/09578239410051844

Rodriguez, A.D. (2014). Culturally relevant books: Culturally responsive teaching in bilingual classrooms. *NABE Journal of Research and Practice, 5*. Retrieved from https://www2.nau.edu/nabej-p/ojs/index.php/njrp/article/view/30/31

Roffey, S. (2012). Teacher wellbeing–pupil wellbeing: Two sides of the same coin? *Educational and Child Psychology, 29*(4), 8–17.

Rousmaniere, K. (1997). *City teachers: Teaching and school reform in historical perspective.* New York, NY: Teachers College Press.

Rubin, G. (2011). *The happiness project: Or, why I spent a year trying to sing in the morning, clean my closets, fight right, read Aristotle, and generally have more fun.* New York, NY: Harper.

Spilt, J.L., Koomen, H.M.Y., & Thijs, J.T. (2011). Teacher wellbeing: The importance of teacher–student relationships. *Educational Psychology Review, 23*(4), 457–477.

Travers, C., & Cooper, C.L. (1998). Increasing costs of occupational stress for teachers. In J. Dunham & V. Varma (Eds.), *Stress in teachers: Past, present and future* (pp. 57–75). London, England: Whurr.

Tyack, D., & Cuban, L. (1995). *Tinkering toward utopia: A century of public school reform.* Cambridge, MA: Harvard University Press.

Valli, L., & Buese, D. (2007). The changing roles of teachers in an era of high-stakes accountability. *American Educational Research Journal, 44*(3), 519–558.

Walsh, B. (1998). Workplace stress: Some findings and strategies. In J. Dunham & V. Varma (Eds.), *Stress in teachers: Past, present and future* (pp. 14–36). London, England: Whurr.

Weber, S., & Mitchell, C. (1995). *'That's funny, you don't look like a teacher': Interrogating images and identity in popular culture.* Washington, DC: Falmer. doi:10.4324/9780203453568

White, P.A. (1992). Teacher empowerment under "ideal" school-site autonomy. *Educational Evaluation and Policy Analysis, 14*(1), 69–82.

CHILDREN'S LITERATURE CITED

Seuss, Dr. (1998). *Hooray for Diffendoofer Day!* New York, NY: Alfred A. Knopf.

SUGGESTED READINGS

Allyn, P., Margolies, J., & McNally, K. (2010). *The great eight: Management strategies for the reading and writing classroom.* New York, NY: Scholastic.

Atwell, N. (1998). *In the middle: New understandings about writing, reading, and learning* (2nd ed.). Portsmouth, NH: Boynton/Cook.

Clayton, M.K. (with Forton, M.B.). (2001). *Classroom spaces that work*. Greenfield, MA: Northeast Foundation for Children.

Cunningham, P.M., & Allington, R.L. (2011). *Classrooms that work: They can all read and write* (5th ed.). Boston, MA: Pearson.

Lambert, R.G., McCarthy, C., O'Donnell, M., & Wang, C. (2009). Measuring elementary teacher stress and coping in the classroom: Validity evidence for the classroom appraisal of resources and demands. *Psychology in the Schools, 46*(10), 973–988.

Marzano, R.J., Pickering, D.J., & Pollock, J.E. (2001). *Classroom instruction that works: Research-based strategies for increasing student achievement*. Alexandria, VA: Association for Supervision and Curriculum Development.

Perrachione, B.A., Rosser, V.J., & Petersen, G.J. (2008). Why do they stay? Elementary teachers' perceptions of job satisfaction and retention. *Professional Educator, 32*(2), 25–41.

Reutzel, D.R., & Clark, S. (2011). Organizing literacy classrooms for effective instruction: A survival guide. *The Reading Teacher, 65*(2), 96–109. doi:10.1002/TRTR.01013

INDEX